Drumming
to the Beat of
Different Marchers

Revised Edition

Finding the Rhythm for
Differentiated Learning

By Debbie Silver
Illustrated by Peter H. Reynolds

Incentive Publications, Inc.
Nashville, Tennessee

Acknowledgement

For their unconditional love and support I would like to thank my Thompson family, my children (Scott, Maverick, Stephanie, Andy, Jeremy, Kandy, and Kit), and my husband/best friend, Lawrence Silver. You are my touchstones and a constant source of joy. Also, welcome to the world, Charlotte Abigail Pace and Gunner Creech Pace!

Illustrated by Peter H. Reynolds
Cover by Peter H. Reynolds
Edited by Jill Norris

Library of Congress Control Number 2005932836
ISBN 0-86530-608-7

PRINTED IN THE UNITED STATES OF AMERICA
www.incentivepublications.com

Table of Contents

Hearing the Drummer

*"If a man does not keep pace with his companions,
perhaps it is because he hears a different drummer.
Let him step to the music which he hears,
however measured or far away."*
—Henry David Thoreau

It wasn't until I started school that I realized I heard a different drummer. I vividly remember my very first day of school. Mrs. Castleberry, my teacher, asked my classmates and me to color a worksheet picture of an apple. I dutifully pulled out my two favorite crayons, green and blue, and laboriously tried to get large chunks of colored wax to stay within the confines of the fruit outline centered on the paper. Not being blessed with well-tuned fine motor skills, my proud strokes made their way beyond the boundaries of the paper itself.

I was quite pleased with my final product—until a dismayed Mrs. C. held up my paper for everyone to see, "Boys and girls, look at this. First of all, apples are NOT blue and green. But more importantly, I said to color **in** the apple, and look what Debbie did . . . she went **outside** the lines!" With a grand show of dismay she wadded up my paper and tossed it in the trash. I can still remember the collective gasps as other students quickly tried to conform their masterpieces to her expectations.

We soon learned that there was to be no *going outside the lines* that year! We were led through a tedious nine-month term of being quiet, sitting still, and repeating exactly what we were told to do. It was not a good year. As one who never made it out of the Slug Group (or whatever insipid name she used for the low readers), I found myself constantly feeling like something was wrong with me.

While some of the students were able to satisfy Mrs. Castleberry's every directive, I was just thankful that I remembered to change my pajama bottoms for real clothes before I showed up at school. I knew the drum I heard was indeed *distant and far away*, but rather than learning to cherish my *outside the lines* thinking, I felt ashamed and frustrated. I remember sitting in the back row thinking, "But I'm smart, too!"

The good news is that there have always been teachers, and later I had some of them, who have the perception, the imagination, and the courage it takes to go beyond the traditional teacher-centered model. They are able to look inside children and see their unique gifts. They differentiate instruction to address the gifts, to engage, to motivate, and to challenge. These teachers don't demand that students march to one inflexible beat; rather, they encourage students to find their own ways, their own rhythms, and their own strengths. They are able to teach students by recognizing and utilizing the gifts they already have.

This book is dedicated to all those teachers who do indeed drum to the beat of their different marchers, and it is written for all those who want to begin.

Part One

Setting the Pace

Chapter 1

Knowing Your Own Rhythm • 11

It is necessary that teachers figure out who they are and determine an educational mission. Then they can set up a classroom conducive to their goals. This chapter offers some food for thought as teachers begin the process.

Chapter 2

Developing a System for Classroom Management • 21

Dealing with classroom management issues is always a key concern for new teachers, as well as those trying to find better ways to create a thriving learning environment. This chapter offers different perspectives on classroom management, as well as many insights about how successful teachers do it.

Chapter 3

Parental Involvement • 59

Keeping pace with individual students is far more expedient and successful when parents are part of the process. This chapter is a guide for getting parents involved and keeping them involved, while not letting them overpower the school's mission or authority. Activities for helping parents deal with their children are included.

Chapter 1

Knowing Your Own Rhythm

If they don't put a nameplate on my door, how will I know who I am?

The Teacher

Concerning a teacher's influence, I have
come to the frightening conclusion that I am
the decisive element in the classroom. It's my
personal approach that creates the climate.
It's my daily mood that makes the weather.
As a teacher, I possess a tremendous power to
make a child's life miserable or joyous. I can be
a tool of torture or an instrument of inspiration.
I can humiliate or humor, hurt or heal. In
all situations, it is my response that decides
whether a crisis will be escalated or de-escalated,
and a child humanized or dehumanized.

—Haim Ginott

Asuccessful classroom environment will be different for different teachers. One classroom does not fit all. Keeping pace with a classroom full of diverse marchers first requires that teachers become acquainted with their own distant drummers. It is important that teachers learn to trust their own "inner voices" and use them to guide all they do. It is vital early on to get a sense of self and a sense of purpose.

Will the Real Teacher Please Stand Up?

When I was in junior high (we didn't have middle schools in the Mesozoic Era), I had a teacher, who shall remain nameless . . . (okay, Mrs. Waggoner). She was just about the meanest, strictest teacher I ever had. She ran her class like a commando camp. We were terrified of her.

One day I had to take a note from one teacher to another teacher who was in the teachers' lounge. I approached with caution fully aware that I was invading sanctified ground. There was so much laughter in the room the teachers couldn't hear me knocking. I opened the door and was struck dumb by what I saw. Mrs. Waggoner was in front of the group royally entertaining everyone. She was laughing and smiling. I almost didn't recognize her with a smile on her face. Feeling like Pandora I ran out of there in a shot! When I told my friends about Mrs. Waggoner's behavior, no one would believe me.

Why were we never given the gift of Mrs. Waggoner's laughter and her humor? Had someone told her, as I was told my first day, that "You can't smile until after Christmas" or "You can always get easier, but you can't get tougher! If you go in there and are nice, those kids will eat you alive!"? Some teachers wrongly assume that they have to fit a certain model in order to maintain control and set up a learning environment. Nothing could be further from the truth.

Be Who You Are!

 This above all—to thine own self be true;
and it must follow, as the night the day,
thou canst not then be false to any man.

—Shakespeare

The greatest gift teachers give to their students is themselves. I think one reason that I did not "burn out" after teaching so many years is that early on I decided to be myself in the classroom, in faculty meetings, at parent conferences, and wherever I was. Unless you are a schizophrenic, it's just too hard to maintain a dual personality. So figure out who you are, and go with it. Just keep getting better at being you.

Researchers have been studying characteristics of effective teaching for the past century. While there are universal qualities regarding a teacher's sense of self and subject matter knowledge that definitely contribute to being an effective educator (Brophy, 1989), there is not research to tell teachers how they ought to **be**.

20 Basic Effective Teacher Qualities

An effective teacher

- is fundamentally a kind, caring person who listens
- possesses a deep understanding of the subject matter
- is self-confident
- believes s/he can make a difference
- has good communication skills
- is creative and interesting
- has an open mind; is willing to try new things
- is generally optimistic and positive
- has a curiosity about the world
- is resourceful
- has a sense of humor
- is flexible
- shows tolerance and is not judgmental
- is able to organize time and materials effectively
- can be described by the students as "with it"
- is energetic and determined
- demonstrates professional and personal integrity
- has patience and persistence
- is willing to "go the extra mile" for students
- acts as an advocate for all students

I am instantly attracted to random teachers who are smart, witty, quick, and entertaining. But some of the most effective teachers I have known have been the quiet nurturers, the deep analytical thinkers, and the highly structured sequential class managers. My point is that once you get past the fundamental characteristics common to all good teachers, the rest is about figuring out who you really are and maximizing those qualities to help you better relate to your students.

It is my belief that if you dance, you should dance with your students. If you can sing, then sing for them. Whether you love to write or play sports or collect things or keep pets, let the kids in on it. Share with them the wonderful qualities that make you who you are. I used to let my students see my old report cards (after I had carefully applied White-Out™ to certain teacher comments about my excessive talking and refusal to follow rules). Students are very curious about you, and letting them in on who you really are will help you build a community of trust and mutual respect. (Use discretion about how much you share. If you supplement your teaching habit by pole dancing at a local honky tonk, you might want to keep that to yourself.)

Promoting a Classroom Community

Careful thought should go into decisions, including those made about what is put in the classroom, how things are arranged, all of the ambient touches added, how rules and consequences are set up, teacher and student attire, the structure of lesson plans, assessment techniques, and virtually everything that has to do with how a teacher chooses to teach.

It took me 10 years of trying various techniques to find a method I really liked for getting the attention of students who were busily working in small groups. I tried counting backwards, flipping the light switch, and whispering. None of those methods

*was satisfactory for me. I finally discovered the
perfect solution in a toy store! I bought a child's
xylophone. It makes a soothing, calming sound, and it gets
the attention of everyone immediately! I've been using it
ever since—even for my university students. I know it
sounds like a little thing, but it has really improved my
classroom environment. It <u>works</u> for me—I just wish I
had thought of it sooner!*

Lion Taming 101

Despite common assumptions, a teacher does not have to meet
students on the first day with a frown, a whip, and an upraised chair in
order to establish order and discipline (even if all the other teachers
are doing it). Students are much better served by a teacher who
greets them at the door, shows them to their assigned seats, and gets
them started on an assignment. Teachers can even smile while doing
all that.

*I often say that my philosophy of teaching can be
summed up in two words: "Whatever works!" Now be
very careful about how this philosophy is interpreted: I
am most definitely NOT talking about stop-gap
measures, arbitrary decisions, or short-term solutions.*

*I show my preservice college students a cartoon of an
unusual classroom scene. In the background is large cage
labeled Mr. Rattles. Inside the cage lurks a huge, fierce-
looking snake. The classroom teacher looks sternly at a
young man and says, "Tommy, I guess you have just earned
yourself ten minutes in the cage."*

My students roar when they see it. Then I ask them, "Would that discipline technique work?" They, of course, tell me that it isn't feasible, not humane, not legal, and so forth. Again I ask, "But would it work? Would ten minutes with Mr. Rattles frighten Tommy into following the rules?" My students usually get a stunned look on their faces and answer that it might, indeed, work.

Then I ask them what they mean by the term "work." Usually they say, "Well, Tommy won't misbehave anymore." It's true. If stopping Tommy's inappropriate behavior was the only goal, it might work. However, making Tommy behave is just one outcome of the many things teachers must consider when making classroom decisions. It is vital that, as quickly as possible, a teacher formulate what he or she believes about the purpose of education and the long-term goals she or he hopes to achieve with students.

The teacher in the cartoon might nip Tommy's behavior in the bud, but has she promoted a classroom that is a caring community? Has she advanced Tommy's requisite knowledge skills? Has she helped Tommy become a contributing member of society? Nope! In order to be truly successful she is going to have to use a better classroom management plan.

Teachers must address key elements when planning classroom management strategies, but classroom management is about much more than discipline techniques. It is about everything teachers do in the classroom. It is important that teachers let their own classroom management style continually evolve until they learn what works. Even learning what not to do ever again is beneficial.

Like the time I jokingly suggested to a very literal student that for his consequence he should, "go play on the little yellow line on the highway in front of the school." Thankfully I caught him before he made it out of the front gate!

All teachers should learn to trust their own *distant drummer*. As a person who has power with children, it is a teacher's obligation to ensure that every decision and action is consistent with what students should know and be like (or are on their way to becoming) when they leave the classroom.

I must be honest and confess that I have probably made every mistake there is to make in managing a classroom. Over the years, I have fluctuated from managing by mood swings (mine) to a diligent application of Lee Canter's Assertive Discipline techniques to Alfie Kohn's absolute classroom democracy plan. None of these systems totally worked for me. However, I did learn from all of them. Talking with other educators and reading about alternative management strategies has helped me reevaluate what I do in my own classes and has given me many new ideas to try.

All teachers learn as they go along. Be patient. It takes more than a year or two to find a personalized path. Some say it takes three to five years for most teachers to *hit their stride*. Teaching is, after all, a faithful work of art and a work of heart.

Chapter 2

Developing a System for Classroom Management

*If they would just get these kids out of my room,
I could probably do my job!*

Dirk's Parents on Discipline
by Debbie Silver

We're here to mention discipline
And how you'll treat our boy;
We want to talk about control
And tactics you'll employ.

We don't believe in violence,
So paddles please don't use.
Don't fuss at him or make a scene,
His ego, it will bruise.

Don't take away his recess time,
He needs a chance to play.
No writing lines or in the hall,
That's wasted time, we say.

We don't agree with contracts made
To punish a misdeed . . .
And don't reward him when he's good,
We think that leads to greed.

So take our Dirk and teach him well,
And our support you'll find.
Oh, yes, and most importantly,
Be sure to make him mind.

Whether one is trying to differentiate instruction in a whole class setting, with flexible groups, or by individual contracts, certain strategies are universally more effective than others. A classroom management plan should be a well-thought-out system that is grounded in recognized behavioral theory. It should be crafted to meet both the short-range goal of having a class run smoothly and the long-range goals of having students become self-sufficient, successful lifelong learners who will become contributing community members.

Beginning and experienced teachers will find a good system of classroom management is grounded on the *The Ten Cs of Classroom Management.*

Effective classroom managers are:

1. Competent
2. Cognizant
3. Communicative
4. Confident
5. Constructive
6. Calm
7. Consistently Fair
8. Caring
9. Contemplative
10. Courageous

On Being Competent

At one time I believed that it was impossible to run an effective classroom without a set of three to five rules. Now, having visited hundreds of classrooms, I have changed that notion. I have been in some highly successful classrooms where there are either no stated rules or the rules are actual governing principles like: (1) Be respectful, and (2) Be responsible. I have seen master teachers who are able to foster such a caring community and such a positive learning environment that rules are replaced with implied standards of behavior and established social mores. To me this is the ideal.

However, for those of us still on the path to becoming true masters, for those who are struggling with difficult students, and for those who are just beginning the journey, I still believe that a written set of rules can be a good place to start.

While there is debate among theorists and educators about the desirability of having a highly-structured assertive discipline plan, there is general agreement that effective classroom rules are a valuable management tool. The carefully-crafted rules should:

- address classroom behavior, not academics
- be applied to all students at all times
- be limited to no more than five in number
- address only the most important behaviors
- be specific and observable
- have logical, consistent consequences
- be reinforced with positive recognition

In his book *7 Habits of Highly Effective People*, Stephen Covey advises that when setting out on a new course of action, one should "begin with the end in mind." This is particularly relevant to classroom management plans. There are two important implications for teachers. First, as teachers craft a plan, it is important to ensure that each rule, each consequence, and each reward is consistent with the long-range goals for students. Second, if using an assertive teacher-centered plan to regain control of an unruly class or to help establish a teacher as a new classroom manager, consider moving away from it as soon as it is comfortable to do so.

As teachers become more confident and more competent, they can aim at building a classroom community that shares more control with students. After all, isn't the ultimate purpose of a discipline plan to help the students develop self-discipline?

T he only way to have true power
is to give some of it away.
— Author unknown

Inexperienced teachers or teachers who are new to a school need to read every word of the school and district handbooks. Highlight important parts and keep them handy. As an employee, a teacher is bound by these guidelines, and it is crucial to understand both the stated and unstated implications of these documents. Beginners will be helped by consulting experienced teachers and/or administrators who can provide feedback on ideas for a classroom management plan. These mentors can also help resolve a conflict with policy or an unforeseen outcome that a new teacher may overlook.

When developing an individual and distinct way of dealing with students, be aware that others may not share the same views. Hearing a different drummer is fine, but a thorough understanding of the issues involved in establishing a positive classroom environment will help teachers defend their choices. I once had an administrator who totally supported classical conditioning as a management technique. He thought that behavior modification was the only way to run a classroom. I had grown to feel that rewarding approved behavior was a bit manipulative and self-serving. Because I keep current with my professional reading, I was able to cite experts who support my beliefs. Sometimes it also takes a little humor to ease your way; I think what ultimately convinced him to let me do it my way was this poem I wrote and placed on his desk:

Ode to Ivan Pavlov

by Debbie Pace (Silver)

Oh, Ivan, you pervade each day
Within my classroom walls—
With one bell ring the students start
Escaping for the halls.

Conditioning cannot be denied
As classic as the text,
Just smelling of the lunchroom food
Will trigger gag reflex.

Mere mention of the "homework" word
Brings on collective bleats.
Appearances by principals
Cause hearts to skip their beats.

You'd think that they'd remember you,
Your work describes them so,
But children learn in unique ways,
As you of all should know.

So, Ivan, I apologize
That when their memory jogs
Their best recall of Pavlov is . . .
That guy with 'slobbering dogs'?

Competent teachers are well-informed both about their subject areas and about how best to deal with their students. A prepared teacher stays up-to-date by reading educational literature, attending workshops, and continually building a repertoire of skills and resources. Expert teachers constantly strive to improve their knowledge base and seek to grow toward an even higher level of competence.

◎ ▦ ◉ ⑪ 🌀 🗋 ◎

On Being Cognizant

Being cognizant means being aware. Often teachers cause their own discipline problems by acts of omission as much as acts of commission. It is not that teachers are uncaring or that they set out purposefully to provoke children, it is that many times teachers are simply not conscious of what they are doing (or not doing). Work on being observant of everything going on in the classroom. Be aware of what students are doing, as well as what they are likely to do. This knowledge can be one of a teacher's greatest management assets. A teacher who is alert to potential problems can head them off before they ever start. Call it being proactive, taking preventive measures, being "with it," or whatever—but do it! Here are four strategies that will help a teacher be cognizant.

Assign Seats

Even though students will later be taught to move efficiently in and out of flexible groups, learning centers, and project areas, it is helpful to assign a default seating arrangement. For this default (or base) seating arrangement, students do not choose their own seats. On the first day students arrive, have them sit in assigned seats. Make folded placards, lay name strips out, or have the seating arrangement posted where everyone can see it. Definitely have it already planned. Explain to the students that the seating arrangement is temporary.

After getting acquainted with the students, reassign their seats.

I take at least as much time filling out my seating charts as I do preparing a lesson plan.

Experiment with different combinations until every student has been given a maximum opportunity to succeed. Move friendly talkers, as well as bitter enemies out of each other's line of sight. Surround particularly argumentative students with several quiet, self-possessed ones. This placement ritual is very cathartic, and it gives teachers a chance to reflect on what's going on with their students.

Whenever changing the base seating arrangement use the magic words **for now** with students. Say something like "These will be your new seats *for now*. We will be changing base seats again in _____ weeks . . ." or "If you are unhappy about your seating assignment, you can write me a note in your journal, but this is your seat *for now*. Let's begin our activity . . ."

Each teacher will have to judge how often to rearrange base seating. A simple rule of thumb is: *the younger the students, the more often changes are needed*. High school students are usually okay with the same seats for one grading period. Middle and intermediate students thrive well with changes every four to six weeks. Let the students know that there is nothing punitive about seating reassignments; it's just beneficial to move them around, so they will have a chance to interact with different people. Some teachers never change students' seats because they think it's too much trouble. Actually, they are missing a golden opportunity to redistribute the power structure in their rooms, take care of minor annoyances, and promote student involvement.

Don't Sit. Move!

As the teacher, it is important to know what is going on among the students. Make sure the seating arrangement allows accessibility to all students. This allows the teacher to monitor, teach, recognize, and affirm individuals. Have students keep traffic lanes uncluttered. Move in an easy, non-threatening manner to different areas of the room at different times.

Also, move in unpredictable directions. This allows teachers to re-engage a dreamer or a drowsy student by moving close to that student and asking a direct question about the lesson.

Students who are trying to confront one another may be glaring at each other. Students may be trying to speak to or entertain one another. Step between them and purposefully engage one or both of them in the lesson.

One of a teacher's best proactive measures is to be able to *move in on* students readily. A lot of acting out can be stopped before it starts by standing close to a student and speaking quietly to the student. Teachers who are standing and moving around have a much better idea about how well a lesson is going and whether the classroom community is functioning positively.

Watch Their Eyes!

 The eyes are the windows to the soul.

This one seems obvious, but many teachers fail to make direct eye contact with students. More can be learned about what is going on with students in a room if a teacher focuses on their eyes. Stand outside the door each time there is a class change. Greet students as they walk in the room. Make eye contact. If a student seems angry or distressed, ask the student to wait in the hall for a moment. While other students are in the room doing their sponge activity (bell work assignment), take a brief moment to find out if the student is going to be able to function in class. It is possible to de-escalate a lot of acting out by showing concern and offering to let the student *cool off* before entering the classroom.

Facilitate lessons by making eye contact to keep students involved. Pay attention to what they are watching. If there is contraband, the students will know where it is, and so will the teacher who watches their eyes.

I know what you're thinking, but I'm just talking about school contraband—gum, candy, water guns, cheat sheets, etc.

If students are behaving inappropriately, capture their attention by looking directly at them. Sometimes no words are needed to redirect their actions; it can all be done with eyes and a slight movement of the head or hand.

A Note About Eye Contact

In many cultures children are taught that it is disrespectful to make direct eye contact with a superior. Be mindful of that and other cultural anomalies when working with children who have different traditions.

Be Knowledgeable About Why Students Misbehave

Teachers must learn about the developmental stages of the students they teach. Some things that students do are simply actions associated with their particular age group. Things like giggling, sulking, acting bored, fidgeting, and other minimally disturbing behavior patterns are typical during certain growth stages.

And, if you think these attributes are particular only to students, check out those who are giggling, sulking, fidgeting, and acting bored at the next faculty meeting.

Understanding the normal phases of the age group being taught will help a teacher to be more patient with student conduct issues.

Be aware that most inappropriate behavior can be attributed to four main causes, and most of the time those causes are preventable. Catherine Watson (1995) states that students misbehave to:
   1) gain power
   2) get attention
   3) seek revenge, and
   4) avoid failure

As teachers move toward a classroom that is more democratic, students will automatically gain more power. The teachers, in turn, will need to encourage positive group dynamics, differentiate instruction, give students more choices about their learning, and engage all learners. Part Two of this book provides background and specific strategies for doing this. Emotionally literate students feel empowered. They are able to find appropriate outlets for the attention they need, and avoid failure. Chapter 8 discusses how to actively promote emotional literacy.

Addressing Watson's third reason is a little more complicated. If a student misbehaves because that student is seeking revenge, the teacher has a serious dilemma. Either this is a student who is extremely troubled, or there is definitely something amiss in the classroom management plan. Teachers should behave toward students in a manner that in no way leads to feelings of revenge-seeking in a normal child. The teacher's role is that of the protagonist, not the antagonist.

Teachers of regular education with students who manifest the need to get even need to take a hard look at what they (the teachers) are doing to trigger such feelings. Obviously there is a deeper problem than just normal *acting out*. It may be that the teacher and the student should meet with a third party to discuss the problem. (Teachers of students who have been identified as emotional behavior disordered, E.B.D., or who have similar exceptionalities are more likely to encounter this phenomenon and should have special training to deal with it when it happens.)

Being cognizant of everything going on is described by some researchers as **with-it-ness**. Being *with it* is an attribute that has been linked to effective teaching (Kounin, 1977). Teachers who are *with it* deter small infractions before they become large ones—the *ripple effect*. They target those responsible for the distraction(s) and redirect attention to the lesson. Good classroom managers are alert, attentive, and able to act quickly.

On Being Communicative

Being able to communicate on all levels with students is crucial to effective classroom management. Teachers who want successful classrooms take time during the first few days of school to teach basic understandings, particularly limits and courteous behavior. They realize that students come to them with different experiences, expectations, and even cultural norms. Often when a student commits some perceived breach of etiquette it is not a result of insubordination, but rather a lack of understanding about what was expected.

> *In the South, children are taught to address their elders by the terms "'Ma'am" and "Sir." Children who transfer into Southern schools from other parts of the country are often misinterpreted as rude or defiant because this is not something they normally do.*

Communicative teachers go over procedures and routines (some call them rituals) in great detail to ensure that all students understand the expectations. In the book, *Discipline with Dignity*, authors Curwin and Mendler suggest that teachers give tests over behavioral expectations. They tie class privileges to making a perfect score on the test, they continue giving the test to those who have not yet made 100 percent, and eventually all students do score 100 percent. Taking time to assess students' understanding of the expected behaviors not only reinforces the ground rules, but it also provides written documentation that the students heard and understood what was expected.

> *Keep that documentation handy for warding off lawsuits from those future attorneys you are now teaching!*

Communicative teachers talk about procedures, demonstrate them, model them, practice them, and revisit them when necessary.

> *Despite what I wrote in the Ivan Pavlov poem, I always taught my students that bells were my signals, not theirs.*

Never let students think that bells, announcements, or departures of other classes dismiss them. The teacher is the one who says when the class is over. On the first day (or any day) if a particular behavior is a problem, stop and address it. Go over the expectations for appropriate conduct again. Have students practice until they get it right. Things will not improve until students internalize the desired procedural behaviors.

Examples of Typical Classroom Procedures:

- lining up for lunch, recess, dismissal, etc.
- drills (fire, tornado, intruder)
- distributing and collecting materials and assignments
- sharpening pencils
- using the bathroom
- tardies
- lunch count
- specialty procedures, like booting up computers, setting up musical instruments, and working in the lab
- moving into and out of flexible groups

When discussing class rules, customs, or standards, effective classroom managers take special care to talk with students about why the policies are in effect. They actively listen to the concerns and opinions of their students. They give their students a voice in the way the class is run.

It is important to note that written rules are not the only way students get messages about what is expected. They watch everything their teacher says and does. Teachers get desired behavior from students by communicating clear expectations to them and following up.

Some teachers still believe that in order to get compliance from children, they have to be unpleasant. Nothing could be further from the truth. At no time should a teacher be aggressive or mean-spirited. Maintain an orderly classroom by communicating in a warm, friendly, and assertive manner. The toughest part for most teachers is being assertive.

Assertive and aggressive are not the same thing. Aggressive means combative, belligerent, and hostile. All aggressive actions are inappropriate in a classroom setting (for faculty as well as students). Assertive means forthright, definite, and positive. When teachers give students definitive expectations and consistently demonstrate that they mean what is said, the students will respond positively.

Some teachers lament, "Well, I have my rules clearly displayed so that everyone can see them, and the students still don't pay any attention to them!" It takes more than writing the rules to get the message across. Inform, model, practice, and continually reinforce the rules.

I was doing a clinical supervision with a novice teacher who had asked me to help her understand why her students did not follow the rules she had on the board. She confided that she used one of the same rules I used—Students will follow directions the first time they are given.—and yet her students wouldn't comply. I sat in the back of her room and observed the following interactions:

MISS WISEMAN (standing in the front of the room with a big smile while students are talking and settling in): Hi, Class! We are going to have a terrific lesson today on what causes an eclipse. Everyone open your book to page 64.

KIT (turning around after talking to a friend during the directions, asking Miss Wiseman loudly): What page?

MISS WISEMAN (patiently): Page 64.

NICOLE (speaking loudly to classmate across two rows): What page did she say?

MISS WISEMAN (answering for the classmate): I said page 64. (She walks over to Nicole's desk and helps her find the page. She then glances around at students still fumbling through their materials. She resignedly walks back to the front of the room and holds up her book for them to see). Students, this is the page I want you to find. (She waits a beat.) Has everyone found the page?

MACKENZIE: I forgot my book.

MISS WISEMAN (becoming frustrated): Okay, then share with Andre. Now . . . (She is interrupted by a loud scraping sound as Mackenzie noisily scoots her chair over to Andre's desk.)

BRIAN (remarking to another student): That's not the right page, you nimrod. We skipped that chapter, remember?

MISS WISEMAN (now really quite agitated): Okay, everyone, STOP! Hold up your hand if you have found page 64 and are ready to go on. I'll wait until all hands are raised . . .

And so it went. Approximate time for Miss Wiseman to start her lesson was six minutes.

During our follow-up meeting I handed Miss Wiseman my scripting notes. I had written only times, dialogue, and actions; there were no evaluative comments. I asked her to look over the script to see if she detected any patterns that might be enlightening. After reading over the events I recorded, she stared at me wide-eyed and said, "I told them to get on page 64 too many times, didn't I?" I let her continue. "I guess if I really want them to listen I should say things just once. But if I do that, some of them will never be on the right page when we start!"

The problem is clear when viewed from the outside. Even though her rule about following directions was prominently written and clearly spoken, Miss Wiseman's words, actions, and tone clearly communicated to her students that she had no expectation of their being able to comply. So many times teachers undermine their own authority by not communicating in every way that they expect students to do what is asked.

It is imperative that teachers tell students about their plan and its purpose. Generally, if a rule is stated, there will be a logical consequence for breaking the rule. Assume that Miss Wiseman's classroom management plan stated that the first rule infraction would mean a check mark by the student's name (as a warning); the second rule infraction would mean a second check mark (two checks = one journal page assignment), and so on.

Now let's assume that Miss Wiseman has already thoroughly discussed her rules and the reasons they are in place. She has explained that her underlying goal is to be sure that in no case will any student be allowed to stop the learning process for others. The purpose of the rule about following directions the first time they are given is to help students take responsibility for their own learning, and to keep the learning process from being interrupted for others.

When they practice the rule about following directions, Miss Wiseman clarifies that if on occasion a student quietly asks for help from another student, or silently moves over to share a book with someone, it will not be breaking the spirit of the rule.

However, if a student speaks out or in any way disrupts the lesson, the rule is clearly broken. The students practice appropriate ways to get help without disturbing others. Then the encounter might go something like this:

MISS WISEMAN (standing in the front of the room with a big smile, and pausing until everyone is facing forward and attentive): Hi, everyone! We are going to have a terrific lesson today on what causes an eclipse. Please open your book to page 64. (She pauses just long enough to give the students time to find the page in their books.)

KIT (loudly): What page?

(Miss Wiseman looks directly at Kit. She lets him see that she is making a check mark by his name on her clipboard. She does not answer the interruption. She goes on with her teaching. Kit realizes what has happened and quickly looks over to another student's book to find the page they are on.)

NICOLE (whispering quietly to a classmate): What page did she say?

(Classmate silently shows her the page, and they both are ready to begin. Miss Wiseman goes on with her teaching. Mackenzie quietly scoots her chair over to a classmate's desk to look on with him. Miss Wiseman asks the class a question about the picture on page 64; all students are engaged in the activity.)

Approximate time for Miss Wiseman to start her lesson: 25 seconds. If Miss Wiseman's goal is to have students behave responsibly rather than just obediently (and hopefully it is), she should be very happy with the previous scenario.

Tips for Effective Communication with Students

- Do not begin instruction until all students are focused and attentive.

- Be sure your voice and body language are consistent with your words.

- Use direct eye contact and simple hand gestures to redirect off-task or inappropriate behavior.

- Use close proximity and a quiet voice to make reminders and censures personal and private.

- Be warm and friendly, and be firm.

- Talk to upset students away from other students.

- Practice active listening skills.

- Write emails, notes, or letters to students occasionally just to tell them why you are glad that you are their teacher.

On Being Confident

There have always been teachers who truly *march to the beat of a different drummer* and are quite satisfied to be who they are. They don't worry about what other people will think or say. They know what they want to do in their classrooms, and they do it. In an effort to do what is best for their students, these teachers take risks and even *color outside the lines*. Studies done on effective teaching have clearly indicated that teachers who demonstrate high degrees of *self-efficacy* are far more likely to have success in their classrooms and in their teaching careers. **Self-efficacy** is a personal belief about one's ability to successfully perform a specific task (Bandura, 1989). The new educational catchword for self-efficacy is **empowerment**. Whatever they're called, teachers' belief systems are powerful predictors of the teachers they will become.

It would be silly for me to tell you, "Just go in there and be confident!" What if you are not feeling very confident? Remember, confidence inspires positive action which invites positive results which reinforces confident behavior. It is a cycle. What you really need is a jumping-in place.

One way to jump into this loop is to act like you feel confident until you do feel confident. I am not telling you to be fake, but I am telling you to put on your best facial expression of capability, stand tall, square your shoulders, speak convincingly, walk forcefully, and try hard to communicate to everyone around you that you believe you can handle everything your job entails. Personally I keep a Super Woman body suit and cape in my teacher book bag for just such occasions.

In theater arts classes they teach actors to emulate the actions normally associated with a particular emotion. When the character is surprised, actors throw up their hands; when the character is sad, actors slump and turn down the corners of their mouths. The actors are much more likely to feel the emotion because actions elicit feelings.

Dale Carnegie said, "Act enthusiastic, and you'll be enthusiastic."
Until you actually feel confident, dress and act confident. Celebrate your own small successes, and find a person on campus who helps you feel as though you can do anything! Actually, you CAN do anything, but you just may not know it yet!

Teachers can help themselves feel more confident by being prepared and by getting to school early. Allow plenty of time to settle in before the students arrive. Teachers gain confidence when they practice exactly what they are going to do and say before class.
One of the student teachers I supervised actually wrote out an entire script for the lesson she was teaching on her observation day. She didn't use it while I was observing, but she said later that just writing it had prepared her and boosted her confidence.
Try making note cards or a checklist. Just do whatever bolsters a feeling of self-assurance.

Teachers should not compare themselves to other teachers. Certainly there will be those with more experience, who are more proficient in certain areas, but overall, each teacher is his or her best.

> *Take the Mirror Test. If you can look at yourself in the mirror at the end of the day and honestly say that you have done the very best that you could under the circumstances, then you have something to be proud of! Play the theme from Rocky throw open your window and yell, "I AM a teacher! . . . or not.*

Confident teachers do not allow themselves to take student achievement or student comments personally.

> *One of my favorite middle school consultants likes to say, "The only reason middle school students come to school is to see who is doing what to whom and what they have on while they're doing it!" So much of what children do and say at school has nothing at all to do with you! They have experiences and agendas so far removed from you that it is really a bit egocentric to think they are out to get you or trying to hurt your feelings.*

Being confident means that individuals are sure enough of who they are that they don't get taken into the students' game playing, name-calling, or passive-aggressive actions. Teachers must separate themselves as the adults. They are professionals who must *rise above the fray*. It is never acceptable for them to be sarcastic or mean-spirited.

Teachers must learn how to become assertive without being hostile. In all cases and at all times, the teacher must quietly, but firmly communicate high expectations for student behavior and give students an opportunity to comply. Always remain calm and professional when addressing inappropriate behavior. When an infraction occurs, it is imperative that the teacher address the behavior and not the child's character.

> *Miss Routt has asked students to open their books to page 64. Kit, who was busy talking to a friend during the direction, asks loudly, "What page did you say? You were mumbling, and I couldn't hear you."*

Read the following three examples of Miss Routt's response to Kit.

A hostile reply:
Miss Routt (sarcastically): "Well, Kit, once again your rude behavior has interrupted this class and made me lose my place! Why can't you follow directions like everyone else?"

A non-assertive reply:
Miss Routt (pleadingly): "Kit, I'll repeat this one more time, but if you keeping blurting out, I am going to have to put a check by your name, okay?"

An assertive reply:
Miss Routt (calmly but firmly): "Kit, you interrupted the lesson." (She puts a check by his name and continues the lesson.)

Teachers must deal with conflict and confrontation as the confident, assertive classroom managers they are. Here are three examples of confident, assertive responses:

- Look a parent in the eye and say, "I am aware of your objections to my discipline plan, Mr. Lindh, and I appreciate your sharing those with me. Please understand that I chose this plan after a great deal of research and thought. So far it is working very well, and my intentions are to keep using it until I find something better. I will, of course, continue to consider options. If you have other ideas for your son's individual plan, I will be happy to discuss them with you."

- Reply to a student inquiring about what happened to another student, "I am going to respect Andrea's privacy on that, Geraldo, just as I would respect yours if and when the situation calls for it."

- Say to the student who is yelling and slamming things around, "You are out of control, Dameon. I am going to call for others to help get you to a place where you can calm down. We will deal with this problem later."

On Being Constructive

School is about building up, not tearing down. Whatever is included in a discipline plan, the positive recognition procedures will be one of its important features. Certainly teachers have to limit choices, attend to disruptive behavior, and ensure that the learning process is interrupted as little as possible. A no-nonsense, firm approach is often needed in such instances. Not everything said and done has to be bright and cheery, but there are many positive, proactive things that can be done to keep a class running smoothly. Just as teachers respond better to affirmative comments rather than negative remarks, so do students.

Many elementary teachers encourage their future students by sending them welcoming letters before school ever starts. I've known middle school teachers who sent *Welcome Back* postcards to all the pupils on their teams. Some of the most effective teachers call parents to report when good things are going on with their children. Effective classroom managers find ways to assure that students receive positive recognition on a regular basis.

One of my favorite methods for encouraging my students is to write a note or letter to them. I've had students who shrugged off my spoken positive comments and praise, but I have yet to have a student return a positive message I have written. For some students my letter is the first such affirmation they have ever received from an adult. Sometimes I thank a child for a specific action such as helping a struggling classmate or backing off from a fight. Other times I tell them that I noticed how hard they are trying or how much their work or behavior has improved. Still other times I tell them what potential I see in them or how glad I am to be their teacher. If the note is sincere and specific, even the most unreceptive students will think about and appreciate what it says.

Tips for Writing to Students

- Write things that are positive and specific to the individual student. Some students will compare their messages to see if the teacher wrote the same thing.

- Make sure everyone gets at least one note from you during the year.

- Be truthful and be sincere. Teachers can even be funny if that's how they interact with students, but be very careful that the words cannot be misinterpreted as sarcastic or negative. Humor is tricky without facial expressions and vocal tone to indicate the writer is joking.

- Make sure the positive comments have no strings attached.

- Don't make a big deal of presenting the note. Be as private as possible. The letter can be mailed.

- Don't ask the student if he or she read the note; give it freely, and let it go.

- Don't ask for, or expect, anything in return.

Let me issue a word of caution on the amount of praise a teacher uses. I learned the hard way that too much praise may create a praise junky! If praise is effusive or indiscriminate, it loses its value to students. Generally, I'm a really positive and verbal person and I truly enjoy giving others tributes, as well as expressing my *appreciation. (I even praise people I don't know. The other day at the airport I told one of the security screeners, "Thank you for helping that lady with her bag. Your mother would be very proud of you.") The point is that in my classroom, my constant compliments soon lost their value. Toward the end of the year, my students would say things like, "Oh, you say that to everybody," or "I'm not going to ask Ms. Silver for her opinion because she likes everything!" It's not easy to find the right balance, but you'll learn to do what works best for you and your students.*

Another warning about praise is that it's self-serving to tie praise to a teacher's approval of what the student does or does not do. Statements like "I'm so proud of you," "I love the way you followed my directions," and "I like the way Tiffany Renee is sitting quietly," subtly tell the children that their goal should be to please the teacher. Just a slight shift of phrasing can give a positive message and help students learn to find approval within themselves, and from adults other than their teacher. The above statements could be changed to "I imagine you feel really good that your hard work paid off." "I'll bet most of you discovered that when you followed directions it made the assignment a lot easier!" "Those of you who are sitting quietly will want to tell your parents how well you listened today."

Are Extrinsic Rewards Constructive?

Along that same line, there is a great deal of argument these days over whether or not teachers should reinforce positive behavior with extrinsic rewards. Purists say that students need to find intrinsic value in the work itself, and that *paying them off* teaches them to work for the reward rather than drawing joy from the experience alone. They cite studies which indicate that intrinsically rewarding behaviors can actually be extinguished if behavior is re-rewarded over a period of time, after which the reward is removed.

Rewards can take many different forms. (Some researchers prefer the term *reinforcers* to the term *rewards* because teachers use them to strengthen or reinforce behavior, thereby making a behavior more likely to be repeated.) The following chart shows five different kinds of rewards:

EXTRINSIC REWARDS	Rewards that come from an outside source such as the teacher. Extrinsic rewards include the obvious bonuses such as certificates, prizes, special privileges, gold stars, stickers, candy, gum, redeemable tokens, grades, or even money. Teacher praise is also considered to be an extrinsic reward, as are more subtle signs of approval such as "thumbs up" signals: smiles, nods, hugs, and pats on the back.
• **Task-contingent Rewards**	Rewards that are available to students for merely participating in an activity without regard to any standard of performance (e.g., a sticker for anyone who turns in a homework paper).
• **Success-contingent Rewards**	Rewards that are given for good performance and that might reflect either success or progress towards a goal (e.g., a sticker for anyone who has at least 95% on a homework paper, or who improves his or her last score by at least 10%).
• **Performance-contingent Rewards**	Rewards that are available only when the student achieves a certain standard (e.g., a sticker for anyone who makes at least 95% on a homework assignment).
INTRINSIC REWARDS	The inherent or natural consequences of the behavior become the reward.

One school of thought argues that anything a teacher does externally to reward student behavior not only robs students of the natural consequences of their choices, it diminishes the students' ability to make independent decisions and robs them of the inherent joy of the experience. On the other side of the argument, it is suggested that teachers have a purposeful, highly visible system of rewarding student choices which are positive. Most researchers agree that task-contingent rewards are at best futile and at worst counterproductive. There are varying opinions about the need for either performance-contingent or success-contingent rewards.

There are reasonable viewpoints advanced by those on both sides. However, there are absolutes on both sides that do not ring true for me. For instance, I am NOT going to teach without smiling, patting, or praising! And I am NOT going to have a no-discretion, no-brain, no-tolerance policy about students being in their seats before the bell rings.

On Being Calm

Once while I was teaching in a large elementary/middle school, I was asked to be a hall monitor during a special Saturday event. Parts of the school had been locked to keep students and visitors out of unsupervised areas. During one of my walk-throughs I spotted four students in an off-limits area. I knew one of them to be a notorious troublemaker and I called for them to stop. When they heard me, they ran. I hurried after them calling more loudly for them to stop. They continued to run, which infuriated me. Despite the fact that I was wearing high heels, I started running full speed after them. I'm quite sure they enjoyed our little chase all over the building because I could hear them laughing.

Finally they got outside and ran into the crowd. I was furious! I stormed into the school office and started yelling that "We have to get those students, NOW!" I was red-faced, out of breath, and out of control.

My principal, who was talking to some parents, excused herself, took me into her office, and asked me to sit down. I was almost hyperventilating at that point. My principal said, "It seems we have a problem."

"Yes," I gasped. "We've got to find those kids NOW!"

"I'm not worried about the kids right now, Ms. Silver, I'm worried about you!"

"Oh, I'll be okay as soon as I get my breath!" I huffed.

"You misunderstand," she said calmly. "I'm worried about how you have chosen to handle this incident. You were running down the halls yelling, then you came into the office and were very unprofessional in front of parents, and now you look as if you are ready to do harm to some of our students."

I was stunned. I was hurt. I was humiliated. I sputtered a moment and then said, "But they were where they weren't supposed to be!"

"I realize that."

"And when I called to them, they wouldn't come!"

"Uh-huh."

"And when I tried to reach them, they ran away!"

"And what did you do at that point?"

"I chased them."

"Why?"

"Because they ran!"

She gently put her arm on my shoulder and said, "Ms. Silver, would you be able to identify any of the students?"

I nodded.

"And do you think that it is highly likely they will be here Monday when we get back to school?"

I didn't say anything.

"And don't you think you could have saved yourself a lot of energy and a lot of embarrassment if you had just written down the names of the students you knew and locked the door behind them?"

She was right, of course. I was so caught up in a swift and just solution (Plus they had royally hacked me off!) that I had lost all perspective.

I have recalled that conversation many times, especially about my answer to her question:

"Why did you chase them?"

"Because they ran!"

How many times do teachers simply react to students rather than act purposefully? If a student can get a teacher to react angrily, the student is the one in control. A student's hostility does not require us to feel likewise. There is absolutely nothing to be gained by getting angry, defensive, hostile, or outraged. Teachers must remind themselves, "I am the adult here. I am the boss of this room."

The older I get, the more I realize how much time I have wasted fighting insignificant battles. Now I save my energy for things that really count. When I am confronted with an insubordinate or *arrogant student I ask myself, "What is my goal here? What can I do to best help this student resolve this situation? Is what I am about to do or say going to help foster the person I want this student to become?"*

Sometimes I realize I am too caught up in the situation to be able to think clearly. Just as my principal taught me, I know that everything does not have to be solved at the moment it occurs. I can distance myself, calm down, think clearly, and address the situation on my terms, not the student's. I don't run after students anymore.

Stephen Covey talks about creating **win-win** situations. Without exception, any time a teacher confronts a student in front of the student's peers, it will never be *win-win*. If the entire class is caught up as the audience in the dramatic power struggle between a teacher and a student, everybody loses.

Let's say that Jerry makes a hostile statement about another student. The teacher asks him to follow the class protocol and apologize. Jerry angrily says, "It wasn't my fault. She started it, and I am NOT going to apologize!"

The appropriate response would be to "move in" on Jerry and quietly say, "Jerry, I need for you to step out in the hall." Then back up and give him room to get out. If he refuses, stay still, remain very calm, and quietly say to another student, "Will you please go to the office and tell them I need help in getting Jerry to step out in the hall." Then ignore Jerry and calmly resume the lesson.

Jerry will probably stomp out of the room before help arrives, but even if he doesn't, remain dead calm! If Jerry does move into the hall, wait for a stopping point, calmly give the other students something to do, then step out into the hall to talk with Jerry. Speak quietly, breathe deeply, move slowly, and do the things people do normally when they are feeling calm. This helps prevent an escalation to anger. Emotions follow actions! Keep focusing on the long-term goals for the class as a whole, and Jerry in particular. If a teacher can do that, everybody wins.

It is also easier to remain calm when realizing that student behavior is seldom attributable to one cause. It usually involves the student's prior experience, his self-perception, his background, his relationships with others in the class, his relationship with his teacher(s), and any number of factors. Be very careful about attributing motive. Remember: students are seldom just out to get their teachers.

Before confronting a disruptive student, teachers must ask themselves these questions:
- Could this be about my own need to win?
- Could I have misinterpreted the situation?
- Have I confronted the one who wasn't the primary instigator?
- Is the hostility which is directed towards me actually displaced aggression?
- Is the student just trying to get attention (even if it is negative)?
- Does the student feel that she or he is not being respected, or is losing face?
- Is it possible that this student really did misunderstand?
- Is this student acting out of a feeling of powerlessness or hopelessness?
- Could this student have been joking?
- Is this student just acting in a way that is typical of his age?

Teachers should apologize when they have misjudged a student, or overreacted in a situation. It is a great object lesson for students to see a teacher admit unfairness, or at least complicity, in the situation. The teacher who apologizes in the appropriate situation earns the respect and trust of students.

If teacher and student are too upset, de-escalate the situation by postponing the confrontation. The teacher might say, "We are both too angry to deal with this now. Let's drop this for the time being and both think about it. Why don't we talk after class?"

If the situation involves a student who has become irrational, calmly say to her or him, "You are out of control right now. I'm going to give you a chance to rein yourself in before I call for assistance."

One special education teacher I know tells students, "We can solve this right now, or others will have to be involved." She confided in me that this always works, and it's a good thing because she has no idea who the others would be. Evidently her students have an ominous view about who the others are!

It can be particularly distressing dealing with group disruptive behavior. Here are some ideas for interventions when several students are involved in the disruption:

- Single out the most powerful offender and deal quietly with her or him.
- Do the *From the Heart* activity (Chapter 7).
- Ask the students to write or draw their feelings and comments.
- Take a time out.
- Do something outrageously silly and laugh.
- Invite others into the room (administrator, grandmother, custodian, older students).

Chapter 7 lists several activities that can be used to build classroom unity and trust. Students can be prepared ahead of time to use conflict resolution techniques. Some schools specifically train certain students to be mediators in difficult situations. It is much easier for teachers to stay calm if they are not the only one who is composed.

On Being Consistently Fair

"Consistent" and "fair" may sound like the same thing, but they are not. In fact they can be mutually exclusive. For example, if the school has a policy of no gum chewing, a teacher can consistently expel children who chew gum. That response is consistent but is it fair?

A second teacher might adjust discipline policy after weighing two factors: first, each individual situation is unique because of the circumstances; and second, each particular student is unique.

Which teacher is right? Should a teacher emphasize consistency or fairness? As much as possible, consider both!

Being consistent builds credibility with students. Giving the mayor's daughter the same consequence given to the disreputable troublemaker for the same infraction lets students know that the rules are for everyone. Enforcing a rule in the last ten minutes of the last period on the day before the Christmas holiday demonstrates that the teacher means what is said.

Consistency with a stated policy helps teachers give comparable consequences for similar breaches without having to think about the decision each time. Teachers should be consistent; however, there is always the danger of becoming robotic and unfeeling when consistency is valued over fairness.

My recommendation is that teachers always err to the side of fairness.

There is nothing so unjust as treating unequals as though they were equal.

In his book *Self-Concept and School Achievement,* William Purkey talks about finding a disclaimer in a drag strip program that states, "Every effort is made to ensure that each entry has a reasonable chance of victory." Purkey believes that it would be a good idea for all schools to follow this maxim.

I agree that the most fair thing we can do in school is to make sure that ALL students feel that there is a reasonable chance for them to succeed!

Otherwise, why should they try? Would you?

As a professional, a teacher should be able to recognize that some students do not have the same level of understanding, the same amount of self-control, nor the same history. Federal Public Law 94.142 stipulates that children identified with special needs cannot be punished for an action caused by their exceptionality (e.g., you cannot punish a child with Tourette's Syndrome for cursing in the classroom). Likewise, there are times that special circumstances for some students (exceptional or not) call for unique and creative solutions to individual behavior problems.

In all cases, make sure that the consequences are logical and reasonable for the behavior breach. A child caught chewing gum loses gum privileges. A child late to class is required to stay after class. Rather than being just punitive, it is helpful if the child actually learns something from the consequence. Students should fill out a behavior journal or individual behavior explanation plan to keep on file. There is an example of a behavior explanation plan on page 196. When a situation is resolved, let it be over. Students should be able to start with a "clean slate" after a consequence has been carried out.

If the classroom policies are working for 24 out of 25 students, should the policies be changed? No. Meet in private with the twenty-fifth student and work out an individual plan for that one student. Say something like, "Stephanie, I see that our management plan is not working for you, so let's come up with something else just for you."

Remember that the teacher is in charge of the room. Each teacher knows better than anyone what will work for his or her students. Do not be afraid to make modifications when the situation calls for it.

Be prepared for other students to cry, "No fair! Why does she have different rules than we do?" One answer is, "I will always try to be fair, but that does not always mean I will be equal." Ask them, "If we all go to the doctor, does he give us all the same medicine? Why not?" "Can all people park in the blue zones? Why not?" Brainstorm with the students to find other examples where fair does not mean equal.

As a teacher builds a reputation among students and parents for being egalitarian, they will question her or him less. It takes time to build a reputation. Be fair and be patient; it will happen.

Over the years most of my students have given me the benefit of the doubt most of the time. When they do question my decisions, I tell them, "I hope that you will trust me enough to believe that I am acting in good faith. You cannot know everything that I know about all the implications involved in this situation. I am the one in charge, and it is up to me to act in what I consider the best interest of all the parties. I will gladly hear your comments and suggestions, and I will make a decision based on the fairest way I know to resolve the issue." And then I do it. (Watch out, Judge Judy, here I come!)

An individualized behavior plan to use or modify as needed can be found on pages 197 and 198. The space for "other" to sign can be signed by parents, a friend, a staff member close to the child, a community member, or whoever else has the respect of the student.

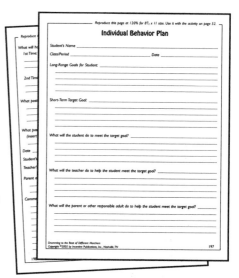

On Being Caring

Our lives are shaped by those who love us (and) those who refuse to love us.

— John Powell

The more time teachers invest in students and the more teachers know about students, the better classroom managers they will be. It is important to know what turns a child on and what turns a child off. On the first or second day of class ask each student to fill out an inventory about themselves. Use the one provided on pages 199–201 or create a new one.

I keep the inventories and periodically go back and read them before creating lessons or making important decisions about dealing with students.

Sometimes teachers make insensitive decisions based not on unkindness, but on inadequate information. Teachers should find out all they can about the lives they touch daily. Drive through the district where students live. Note the exteriors of the homes, the vehicles parked around, and the general "feel" of the neighborhood. Make every effort to understand the students' culture. Watch what they watch on TV. Listen to their music. Talk to them. Find out the amount of time each child spends on the bus each day. What time do they have to get up to catch the bus? What time do they get home in the afternoon?

Knowing these things can help a teacher make more appropriate homework assignments, affect comments, and guide expectations. It is important to balance an understanding of the students' problems with clear statements of acceptable behavior choices. Students do not need for teachers to pity them, but they do need for teachers to understand them. Having an informed view of their lives bolsters a teacher's commitment to keep expectations high, but reasonable.

A Note About Physical Contact

Teachers are often told that in these days of paranoia and unrestricted litigation, it is best never to touch a child for any reason. I just cannot and will not support that notion. Some children are starved for appropriate human touch. I believe that teachers who feel comfortable hugging, patting, and otherwise affirming children should do it! Of course, be cautious if the situation warrants it.

Be aware of the community norms and situations that are questionable. When in doubt, talk with a respected administrator or colleague. Respect the student's limits; some students do not want to be touched at all. (They may have been harmed and are distrustful of adults.) Never touch a student in anger or to restrain her or him unless there is a safety issue. Keep physical contact as well all things in the classroom, consistent with the long-term goals. When used wisely, the human touch is a powerful complement to caring. Above all, maintain the child's dignity.

On Being Contemplative

Being contemplative means that teachers should spend time and energy thinking about how to improve their techniques and strategies. Expert teachers did not become experts overnight. They tried new things, made mistakes, had successes and failures, reflected on the results, decided what to keep and what to toss, and repeated the process over and over again. It's a little like mastery learning. A learner gets one part right and then the teacher builds on it. The key is for teachers to be constantly thinking about what they are doing and why they are doing it. Read, study, and think deeply about how it all fits together.

Whether headed by a novice or an experienced educator, a classroom will run better in direct proportion to the amount of time spent planning, preparing, and reflecting. Contemplative teachers plan, prepare, and reflect so that when almost any situation comes up they have considered the consequences to their responses in advance. Use the following set of planning principles.

Contemplative Teachers Plan How They Will:

- react to different situations
- reinforce positive behavior
- extinguish negative behavior
- individualize discipline practices for difficult students
- engage all learners
- differentiate instruction for diverse learners
- foster a classroom community
- build their own resiliency so that they will be at their personal best

Engaging learners and differentiating instruction are discussed throughout Part Two of this book. Keep in mind that they are integral parts of a functioning management plan. Discipline works best when associated with good instructional methods and good assessment methods. Rules, consequences, and rewards cannot be isolated from everything else that goes on in a classroom. Instruction, classroom management, room environment, and planning all work together. Discipline problems will be kept to a minimum when students are actively engaged and given the chance to feel successful in their work. As teachers learn more about their subject areas and the culture of their students, they become more adept at utilizing good instructional techniques to help avert discipline problems.

Today more than ever, educators must focus not only on cognitive issues, but also on the emotional literacy component of learning and working together. *That's what Baby Boomers used to call the "affective domain," and some naysayers still call "that touchy-feely-I-need-to-validate-my-feelings stuff."* Successful students live meaningful, productive lives; they do not just achieve a certain score or grade.

The eighth C of classroom management simply means, the better teachers think, plan, prepare, and take care of themselves, the better they can teach others. Period! Effective teachers spend hours in preparation and contemplation. They learn from their mistakes, continue to consider ideas, try new things, and constantly ask themselves, "Is this working?" and "Will this foster in students what I believe they need for lifetime goals?"

Schools are not isolated entities. Forces outside the school shape the way things go inside the school. Become familiar with what those forces are and change the things you can change. Accept the things you cannot change, and do your best to work around them. Remember that some students may need more than any teacher can give. Involve others when necessary. Do what is possible, and always leave the door open.

On Being Courageous

New teachers need to be told, "Remember always: YOU ARE THE BOSS OF YOUR ROOM!" No one should tell a teacher otherwise. In the end, it is the teacher who is accountable for everything that goes on in that classroom. Teachers have every right to say what is acceptable and what is unacceptable in their own classrooms.

Teachers do not have the right to say to students, "That kind of language is gutter filth! You are going to go straight to Hell if you continue to talk like that!" But they do have the right to say, "That kind of language is not appropriate for this classroom. Don't use it in here."

Teachers have a responsibility to demand respect for themselves and for all the students! Teachers also must maintain a safe and secure environment for themselves as well as for their students. Do whatever it takes to achieve these conditions.

Sometimes a teacher may be criticized by colleagues for not *going along with everybody else*, or *for making the rest look bad*. Parents may say,

> "Well, that's not the way Mr. Socrates did it!"

or

> "You are obviously unaware that our brother-in-law is on the school board!"

It takes courage to march against the ranks, but if it is right for kids, do it!

Never forget that schools are first and foremost for the students! In all cases teachers must be an advocate for children. So many kids today do not have a voice. Many are abused, afraid, ignored, angry, hurting, confused, and/or at risk in some way. Teachers must speak out for their best interests.

Recommended Reading List

Burke, Kay. *What To Do with the Kid Who . . .* Arlington Heights, IL: Skylight Professional Development, 2000.

Canter, Lee, and Marlene Canter. *Lee Canter's Assertive Discipline: Positive Behavior Management for Today's Classroom.* Santa Monica: Lee Canter & Associates, 1992.

Canfield, Jack, and Howard Clive Wells. *100 Ways to Enhance Self-Concepts in the Classroom.* 2nd edition, Englewood Cliffs, N.J.: Pearson Education, 1994.

Covey, Stephen R. *The 8th Habit: From Effectiveness to Greatness.* New York, NY: Free Press, 2004.

Curwin, Richard L., and Allen N. Mendler. *Discipline with Dignity.* Alexandria, VA: Association for Supervised Curriculum (ASCD), 1988.

Glasser, William. *Control Theory in the Classroom.* NY: HarperCollins, 1986.

Glasser, William. *The Quality School: Managing Students without Coercion.* 3rd edition, NY: Perennial, 1998.

Kohn, Alfie. *Beyond Discipline: From Compliance to Community.* Alexandria, VA: ASCD, 1996.

Kohn, Alfie. *Punished by Rewards: The Trouble with Gold Stars, Incentive Plans, A's, Praise, and Other Bribes.* Boston: Mariner Books, 1999.

Wormeli, Rick *Day One & Beyond: Practical Matters for New Middle-Level Teachers.* Westerville, OH: National Middle School Association, 2003.

Chapter 3

Parental Involvement

If it weren't for the parents, we wouldn't have all these kids in the first place!

Roses

by Timothy Gallaway

When we plant a rose seed in the earth, we notice that it is small, but we do not criticize it as "rootless and stemless." We treat it as a seed, giving it the water and nourishment required of a seed.

When it first shoots up out of the earth, we do not condemn it as immature and underdeveloped; nor do we criticize the buds for not being open when they appear. We stand in wonder at the process taking place and give the plant the care it needs at each stage of its development.

The rose is a rose from the time it is a seed until the time it dies. Within it, at all times, it contains its whole potential. It seems to be constantly in the process of change; yet at each state, at each moment, it is perfectly all right as it is.

There was a time in American education when schools could count on parents for almost total support. Most students came from two-parent homes where schools were regarded as sacrosanct. Today's parents, on the other hand, may be single mothers, single fathers, stepmothers, stepfathers, grandmothers, significant others, newly-arrived immigrants, affluent, middle class, or impoverished.

> *I was quite shocked the first time I realized that some*
> *of the parents of my students were little more than*
> *children themselves!*

The term *parent* can be used broadly to include the wide range of important adults in a child's life. In this chapter the term is referring to the primary caregiver or person most responsible for the child's well-being, education, and development.

The issue of how important it is to involve the students' parents goes back to the guiding principle teachers must use for everything in education. What is the best way to ensure that both the short-term and long-range goals for students are met? In all cases, educators are better able to meet the needs of students if they have parents on their side. Therefore, teachers have to do everything possible to engage the parents as active participants in their children's education.

Research Supports Parent Involvement

In their National Standards for Parent/Family Involvement Programs, the National Parent Teacher Association (1997) cites research that clearly indicates:

1. When parents are involved, students achieve more, regardless of socioeconomic status, ethnic/racial background, or the parents' education level.

2. The more extensive parent involvement is, the higher student achievement will be.

3. When parents are involved, students exhibit more positive attitudes and behavior.

4. Children from diverse cultural backgrounds tend to do better when parents and professionals collaborate to bridge the gap between the culture at home and the learning institution.

5. Secondary students whose parents remain involved make better transitions, maintain the quality of their work, and develop realistic plans for their future. Students whose parents are not involved are more likely to drop out.

6. The most accurate predictor of a student's achievement in school is not income or social status, but the extent to which that student's family is able to:

    a) create a home environment that encourages learning

    b) communicate high, yet reasonable expectations for their children's achievement and future careers, and

    c) become involved in their children's education at school and in the community

Even though research has overwhelmingly demonstrated that the greatest predictor in a child's success in school is associated with the home factor, many teachers are hesitant to reach out to parents. They are sometimes stymied by the implied **Myth of the Good Teacher**, which is the belief that really talented teachers never have to ask for help, or that teachers who truly do their jobs well require no other adult assistance for a smooth-functioning classroom.

That notion is as absurd as it is harmful. Teachers have a right to have parental support, but they also have a responsibility to ask for and expect it. No matter how talented teachers are, they cannot provide the extended one-on-one time with a child that parents can.

Parental approval is a powerful motivator for students. A lack of participation on the part of the parent sends a message to the child that he or she is not worth the effort. An involved parent can provide the directed practice a child needs for mastering certain skills, as well as encouragement for a lifetime of success. Never forget that parents are the most important, influential people in a child's life. Teachers cannot do their jobs effectively without them.

> The best inheritance parents can give their children is a few minutes of their time each day.
>
> — Author unknown

There are effective techniques teachers, as individuals, can employ to involve the parents of the students they teach. The key phrases to remember are *communicate, problem solve,* and *enlist support.*

Communicate with Parents

Start early communicating with parents. Before school starts, or on the first day of school, make contact. Teachers should introduce themselves with a letter, and let the parents know that they want to work together to help their child have the best year possible.

Give the parents an overview of the class plan and expectation. Parents will recognize the planning and expertise reflected in the plan. Provide a translation for parents who have limited use of English. Let them know how important they are in the ultimate success of their children's lives. Always demonstrate respect for the family and the family's primary role in helping students become responsible adults.

Be friendly, be professional, be inviting, and be sure all written communications use correct grammar and punctuation!

I promise you that if you don't, someone will correct it in red and send it back!

Use an informal font or clip art to make the letter seem less officious. Give parents contact information, and invite them to use it.

Make the first move. Do not wait for the parents. If teachers care about what happens to their students, they have to involve themselves with parents. Set the tone for the school year, make the first parent contact a positive one! As the year continues, keep in touch.

Here are the top ten ways teachers communicate with parents:

Top 10 Ways to Keep in Touch With Parents

- Phone
- Email
- Voice mail
- Fax
- Web site (school or class)
- In-person contacts
- Newsletters
- Academic calendar
- News bulletins/community bulletin boards
- Notes and cards (If all else fails, send parents a registered letter.)

Problem Solve and Enlist Parental Support

 Anyone who says, "easy as taking candy from a baby" has never tried it!

— Author unknown

In every communication teachers have with parents, the ultimate goal is to help the student. Teachers who are at cross-purposes with parents cannot help students. My best piece of advice about dealing with parents is to treat parents as you want to be treated. That sounds really simple, but sometimes parents make it difficult to be that compassionate. Once in a while, after an unpleasant encounter with parents it may appear that the student would fare much better as an orphan. However, never underestimate the power of parents!

Dealing with parents can tax a teacher's best interpersonal communication skills. Even expert classroom teachers often shy away from encounters with parents. It may be helpful for teachers to practice role-playing with a group of colleagues. Ask an administrator if a faculty meeting could be devoted to having teachers practice their parent-conferencing skills. Experienced teachers can be a big help in supplying neophytes with strategies and phrases that will help them remain compassionate and in control.

Tips on Problem Solving with Parents

- Keep parents up-to-date on what is going on with their child. If grades or behavior take a downward plunge, let the parents know immediately. Parents do not like surprises! An often-repeated question parents ask is, "Why didn't I know about this sooner?" Indeed, why didn't they? There is little defense for not alerting parents to potential problems. There is often a good chance they can help prevent the bigger problem.

- Do communicate what is happening in the classroom. Whether it is changing the discipline plan, initiating a new test policy, or planning a field trip, parents want to know what is going on. Tell them. Do not be defensive! Let parents know that their child's teacher is in charge and capable. Explain policies and procedures, but do NOT apologize for them.

- Do not attempt to solve problems at chance encounters with a parent or guardian. The grocery store check-out line, the school football game, or the church parking lot are not locations conducive to a professional meeting. Have the parents come to school at a scheduled time. Focus on the parents and have ready access to your grade book and the student's work.

- Establish a common ground with parents. Both teacher and parent are there to act in the best interest of a child. Even if a teacher and the parents have to *agree* to *disagree* on an issue, find commonality in the commitment to the student's welfare.

- Expect parents' full support. Speak to parents as equals in the problem-solving process. If they come to school to talk, sit beside them in adult chairs. Do not apologize for bothering them at home or at work. When acting on their child's behalf, no apology is needed.

- Help parents identify the specifics of the problem. Show them documentation whenever possible. Make notes as they supply information or ask questions. Write down the plan of action agreed to and give them a copy.

- Give parents very concrete, specific ways to help. Some of their most important contributions can be very simple—turning off the TV (also CD players, computer games, and cell phones), instituting a quiet study time, making sure the child has a place to work, and asking them to look at completed assignments.

- Try to say to the parents early in the conversation, "But I'm sure I'm not telling you anything that you don't already know."

    I nod my head while saying, "I'm sure you see the same behavior at home, right?" Before they know it, they are nodding right along with me and admitting that the problem is not unique to my classroom.

- Ask for and listen to parents' advice about how to handle situations with their child. Questions such as "How do you deal with it?" and "What is working for you?" help parents to think about solving the problem, rather than defending the behavior.

- Be empathetic and compassionate, but stick to the subject. Don't let the parent wander off into areas that have no solution or no relevance. Avoid blaming. Gather as much information as possible.

- Provide a follow-up plan to check on progress. End the meeting by recapping the important points and setting a time to be back in touch.

- Be alert to common excuses and ploys:

    - *"Oh, none of us Johnsons has ever been very good at math." That's either a rationalization for not dealing with the inadequacy or guilt for not having addressed it earlier. Accept their explanation non-judgmentally, but keep moving them toward a solution.*

    - *"She doesn't listen to anything I say. I tell her to turn off the TV and study, but she won't." Bolster the parent's responsibility and inevitable accountability. Offer to bring in outside resources. Give positive suggestions and hold your ground!*

- Occasionally a teacher will encounter parents that give the teacher *carte blanche* privileges to discipline their child. Rather than seeing this as supportive, acknowledge it for what it is: an abdication of the parent's obligation to help the child extinguish inappropriate behaviors. They are asking the teacher to act in their stead rather than deal with the unpleasant task of enforcing rules and following up with consequences.

- Understand that some problems are simply too overwhelming or too disturbing for parents. Assure them that even serious problems have solutions. Suggest other experts to help deal with the problem.

- Remember that educators are required by law to report incidences of child abuse. Period. It is not only a moral issue, but also a legal one. A teacher who is suspicious (but not sure) should consult a counselor or an administrator. Carefully document all suspected occurrences.

- Finally, when communicating with parents, do not use jargon and definitely try to keep your sense of humor!

۝ ۝ ۝ ۝ ۝ ۝ ۝

Too Much Parental Support?

Parental support isn't just about baking cookies or chaperoning the class party anymore. Some parents are asking to be more and more involved in decisions dealing with curriculum, schedules, school policies, and virtually all aspects of the educational community. Sometimes there is a fine line between supporting the school's purpose and getting in the way of it.

Usually a workshop on parental involvement is given in response to low or nonexistent parental support However, there are occasions when teachers and administrators have the opposite problem. They feel that their parents are too involved and/or overpowering. There are some situations where a parent seems to have become a *Professional Michael's Mom* or a litigious *Anna Advocate*.

> *I have heard some educators say that they would rather have parents be totally inattentive than for them to be "over-involved" with their children's education. I disagree. I find that it is easier to divert excessive attention than it is to generate it when there is little or none to begin with. At least the disproportionately attentive parent is interested in his or her child's welfare.*

If dealing with a parent who is usurping a teacher's authority or becoming over-involved in classroom operations, these strategies will help.

Dealing With An Over-Involved Parent

1. Be proactive. Invite their involvement when it is convenient for the teacher.

2. Ask the parent to volunteer in classes or areas other than those his or her child attends.

3. Dilute their power by asking under-represented groups to serve on committees, chair events, and volunteer with them.

4. Steer them towards working for the benefit of all students, and sincerely praise their efforts. (Many times these folks are just starved for attention or for the chance to contribute something meaningful.)

5. Clearly identify their limits. Let them know the teacher is in charge and has ultimate veto power.

6. Be cautious about sharing information regarding other students, faculty, or administrators. Non-school personnel should not be privy to any confidential information. Gossip is a huge (and extremely unprofessional) no-no!

7. Keep a sense of self; do not be caught up in parent agendas.

8. Invite them to help get other parents involved.

9. Remind them that it is natural to want a child to do his or her best, but it is unfair and unrealistic to ask her or him to be the best.

10. Always maintain a sense of humor. (Sooner or later children move on, and so do their parents.)

Helping Parents with Parenting Skills

Some members of our profession lament, "It's not my job to teach these parents how to be parents! It's all I can do to teach their children!" I realize that teachers are asked to assume far too many duties and responsibilities as it is. However, I often ask myself and my colleagues, "If we don't do it, who will?"

Occasionally, a parent just needs a listening ear or the reassurance that the child's behavior is a normal developmental stage and will soon pass. Sometimes a teacher can give them the gift of pointing out strengths in their child they had not before recognized (most of them associated with Gardner's 8 Levels of Intelligence). Professional resources may help teachers address common problems. One source is a collection of information sheets for parents published by the National Association of Elementary School Principals (NAESP). Their members receive a regular supplement (written both in English and Spanish) called **Report to Parents**. Educators are invited to include the reports with their school newsletters to parents. NAESP gives full permission for the pages to be reproduced. Current topics such as bullying, child safety, over-scheduling children, children and drugs, antidotes for violence, TV watching, and other timely topics are covered in a simple, applicable style. These supplements make excellent starting points for teacher-parent communications.

I have encountered family problems that are far beyond the scope of my expertise or training. In those cases, I am quick to refer parents to more qualified professionals. However, I find that many parents are simply asking my advice on how they can be better parents.

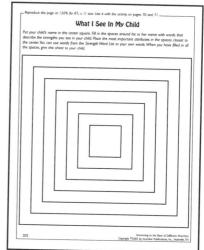

For parents who are particularly negative or critical of their children, ask them to focus on their children's strengths. Reproduce and provide the parents with a blank form (page 202)

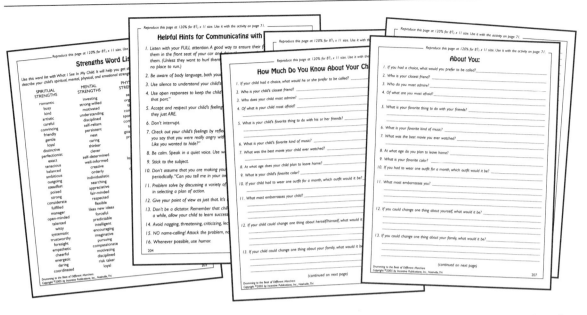

and a list of strengths (page 203). Have the parents focus on the positive side of their child as they complete the form. The result can be very illuminating to negative parents.

For parents who are having a tough time communicating with their children, provide the tip sheet *Helpful Hints for Communicating with Your Child* on page 204.

To open the lines of communication between parents and their children, administer the following interest assessment. Ask parents and students to go to different rooms or to different areas of the same room. The parent questionnaire is found on pages 205 and 206. The student questionnaire is on pages 207 and 208. Reproduce the forms and have parents and students simultaneously fill out the assessment. After both have finished, they should score the assessment together and hopefully engage in some meaningful discussions.

Teaching children does not happen in a vacuum. So much of what goes on in class reflects what goes on in the community, that it is ridiculous to try and separate the two. Building an alliance with parents and the rest of the community is one of the best practices educators have for ensuring that both short-term and long-range educational goals for children are met.

Recommended Reading List for Educators

Beckwith, Harry. *Selling the Invisible: A Field Guide to Modern Marketing*. NY. Warner Business Books, 1997.

Canter, Lee, and Patricia R. Sarka. *Parents on Your Side*. Santa Monica: Lee Canter & Associates, 1991.

McEwan, Elaine K. *How to Deal with Parents Who Are Angry, Afraid, Troubled or Just Plain Crazy*. Thousand Oaks, CA: Corwin Press, 2004.

Pelzer, David. *A Child Called "It": One Child's Courage to Survive*. Deerfield Beach, FL: Sagebrush, 1999.

Stepp, Laura Sessions. *Our Last Best Shot: Guiding Our Children through Early Adolescence*. NY: Sagebrush, 2001.

Whitaker, Todd C. *Dealing with Difficult Parents (And With Parents in Difficult Situations)*. Larchmont, NY: Eye on Education, 2001.

Recommended Reading List for Parents

Berckemeyer, Jack and Patti Kinney. *The What, Why, & How of Student-Led Conferences.* Westerville, OH: National Middle School Association, 2005.

Cooper, Nic and Rick McCoy. *How to Keep Being a Parent . . . When Your Child Stops Being a Child.* Canton, MI: Willow Creek Publishing, 1999.

Covey, Sean. *7 Habits of Highly Effective Teens.* NY: Fireside, Inc., 1998.

Hallowell, Edward M., and John J. Ratey. *Driven To Distraction. Recognizing and Coping with Attention Deficit Disorder from Childhood through Adulthood.* NY: Touchstone, 1995.

Shedd, Charlie W. *You Can Be a Great Parent!* Waco: Word Books, 1970.

Salt, J. S. *Always Kiss Me Good Night. Instructions on Raising the Perfect Parent by 147 Kids Who Know.* NY: Three Rivers Press, 1997.

Shapiro, Lawrence E. *How to Raise a Child with a High E.Q: A Parent's Guide to Emotional Intelligence.* NY: HarperCollins Publishers, Inc., 1998.

Part Two

Differentiating Instruction

Chapter 4

Teaching Those Who Hear Different Drummers • 79

In a learning cycle lesson, students are asked to develop their own understandings through exploration, investigation, and participation. Carefully guided questioning and application of newly learned skills yield knowledge that is extremely personal and meaningful. This chapter explores the learning cycle, a constructivist approach to teaching and learning.

Chapter 5

Multiple Intelligences and Different Learning Styles • 101

All students learn; but it is important to recognize that they learn at different rates and in different ways. The teacher's job is to capitalize on students' natural strengths to help them find their own best means for learning. This chapter focuses on brain research about multiple intelligences, learning styles, and flow state.

Chapter 6

Learning to March in Formation—Cooperative Learning • 127

The use of small group interactions in learning situations can lead to higher-order thinking, enhanced feelings of individual self-esteem, and greater academic achievement. Cooperative learning is an effective instructional and assessment strategy that can improve student learning and promote emotional literacy among peers.

Chapter 4

Teaching Those Who Hear Different Drummers

Get out your training wheels and prepare to ride the learning cycle.

Science Students' Misconceptions
by Debbie Silver

Children learn in unique ways,
Their own ideas they bring—
Like, "When the sun moves toward the earth,
Now, that's what causes spring!"

They think inertia just applies
To objects as they move.
They won't believe in infrared
No matter what you prove.

They're positive that switches store
All electricity.
And friction's not on things real smooth—
Just ask them, you will see.

The North Pole is Magnetic North,
The kids are sure it's so.
To misconceptions they do cling
To prove the things they know!

Most misconceptions must be faced,
(But some of them are fine . . .
Like when my students guess my age,
"Ms. Silver's thirty-nine!")

T he single most important factor influencing learning
is what the learner already knows."

— David Ausubel

T he *industrialized* version of what education should be is firmly grounded
in the R³ method—read, recite, and regurgitate. This style is expedient,
easily replicated, and most effortlessly assessed. Designers of this
methodology purposefully avoided having a system that required teachers to
be creative, intuitive problem-solvers. Their belief is that instructors cannot be
trusted to make decisions based on the individual needs of children. They
want a curriculum that is *teacher-proof*, and in the process they have fostered a
league of educators who are *student-proof*.

If it's so evident that this is not the best way for students to learn, why
don't all teachers change their methods? For some it is extremely difficult to
break with a tradition that is so deeply ingrained in the institution of school.
The reality is that teachers live in a standards-based world in which accountability often means that students are required to demonstrate common literacy
and skills acquisition. Students enter school with different knowledge levels
resulting from diverse experiences, backgrounds, and cultural values. Teachers
must take these factors into account and present new information in a

meaningful way appropriate to each learner's existing knowledge. The task can seem daunting, but there is a relatively simple lesson design that has been used successfully by teachers across disciplines and for all grade levels to accomplish this end. It can be used to help differentiate instruction in a whole class setting or in smaller groups.

R aise new questions
    Explore new possibilities
        Regard old problems from a new angle.

                    — Albert Einstein

Engaging the Learner and Making Connections

One of the concerns of traditional educators is that teaching *those who step to different beats* will take away time and other resources better spent getting as many students as possible to pass standardized tests.

> *Without going into an argument about the legitimacy of teaching to a test, let me just say that assessing for true understanding has little to do with merely acquiring isolated facts of content knowledge.*

More and more educators today view "teaching" as an interactive verb that requires the engagement of the learner as well. A teacher may say it, write it, demonstrate it, or in any other manner make a sincere effort to convey it to students, but if the students do not learn it, it cannot be said that the teacher taught it. Thus, the focus today is shifting away from teachers being the gatekeepers of all knowledge and rules, to one in which the teacher interacts with the curriculum and the students by planning interactive learning tasks, designing more authentic types of assessment, and redirecting time and energy (Vatterott, 1995).

What would happen if all teachers began to *drum to the beat of their different marchers* instead of forcing all students into the same-paced, teacher-centered instructional model? In a study conducted by a superintendent, school principals were assigned to shadow 45 students in nine different settings. Among other things, they reported that most of the classes they observed were boring and not engaging. They found a disproportionate number of African-American and Hispanic students placed in special programs. They reported scant evidence that participation in programs for mildly handicapped students had benefit. Despite these findings, their school district was eventually able to improve overall test scores and morale by including more special education students in regular education classes and promoting a more constructivist curriculum for all students. (Lytle, 1996).

Unless students can balance their experiential knowledge with newly presented information, they will not be able to learn it and use it. Piaget (1974) described this occurrence as "finding equilibration through accommodation and assimilation of new information." Effective teachers have always been able to engage their students by relating what was to be learned to what they already knew. They seem to have a sense of where their students are in their understandings and, armed with that knowledge, they virtually *go in after them.*

These educators realize that students can better construct new meanings by actively seeking to make sense of things on their own rather than having the lessons presented in an already established format. Instruction begins by purposefully addressing students' predisposed misconceptions.

In her 1999 book *The Differentiated Classroom: Responding to the Needs of All Learners*, Carol Ann Tomlinson concurs that a classroom that is healthy for learners is characterized by the fact that what is taught and learned:

- is relevant to students; seems personal, familiar, and connected to the world they know
- helps students understand themselves and their lives more fully now, and will continue to do so as they grow up
- is authentic, offering real history or math or art, not just exercises about the subject
- can be used immediately for something that matters to the student
- makes students more powerful in the present, as well as the future

For educators who are discouraged by all the latest and greatest trends we have endured in education, let me assure you that I am not talking about an abandonment of all that has previously been taught. Actually, all that really needs to be done is to shift the responsibility of learning onto students rather than expecting teachers to provide all the informational output.

Traditional textbooks had a set format. They started with a list of the new vocabulary words, a fact list, and an introduction of the topic. Next there were lots of examples and rules followed by skill development practice exercises. Then there was the objective end-of-the-chapter test. At the very end of the chapter there were some really thought-provoking activities and discrepant events. They were given a title like *For Enrichment and Going Further.*

Most of my teachers let only the early finishers attempt those activities.. Looking back, I realize that if my teachers had started with the fun, challenging activities, as a student I would have been much more likely to have responded to the rest of the lesson.

Luckily, many textbooks today are written from a **learning cycle** perspective. Often they start each new lesson with a discrepant event, an interesting link, or a thought-provoking question. However, teachers do not need to be slaves to textbook writers. Any core or encore curriculum can be adapted to meet the learning cycle model.

Teaching is an active verb that requires the engagement of the learner. Because it has become harder and harder to capture the attention of students, *discrepant events* are a way to stimulate interest in a particular topic. For instructional purposes, a discrepant event can be described as an investigation in which the new information that is introduced is inconsistent with information previously thought to be true (misconceptions). Piaget referred to this type of learning when he described how learners can be motivated to learn if they experience a sense of "disequilibration."

As long as the learner's environment is stable, mental activity is not necessary. But when an unfamiliar problem arises the learner must use prior experience, new insights, and/or peer interaction to solve the problem and reestablish equilibration. Equilibration can be restored through *accommodation,* whereby the learner creates or restructures his or her thought patterns, or through *assimilation,* whereby the learner incorporates the new information into existing thought patterns. A discrepant event can arouse interest and allow for exploration, discovery, questioning, and discussion. This involvement and interaction between students and their environment will initiate linking and application. Discrepant events can be used to help students learn.

Learning is finding out what you already know.
Doing is demonstrating that you know it.
Teaching is reminding others that
they know it just as well as you.
You are all learners,
doers, teachers.

— Richard Bach

Understanding the Structure of the Learning Cycle

Teachers can use the instructional model called *the learning cycle* to help children make sense of their worlds. Instructors of all levels and all subjects can modify traditional lesson plans so that no student is left behind.

When using the learning cycle, lessons begin with what students already know. Learning cycle lessons are intentionally designed to give all learners, the Melissas and the Julies, a reasonable chance at success. Read *Queen of the Teeter-Totter* on the next page for a concrete example.

Queen of the Teeter-Totter

By Debbie Silver

Melissa's in the upper group,
A verified class leader.
Little Julie sits in back,
A proven low non-reader.

> The teacher has them open texts
> To read about a lever.
> She tells them they must learn the facts
> To be a high achiever.

Melissa does her worksheet fast,
She writes each definition.
But Julie mixes up the words,
And gives up in submission.

> "Poor Julie," says the teacher then,
> "You cannot do this science.
> With our state's standards as they are,
> You'll never make compliance!"

She sighs and sends the kids to play
Melissa leads them proudly,
"I made the best grade in the class,"
She tells the others loudly.

> But on the playground Julie reigns
> She rules the teeter-totter.
> She strands Melissa in mid-air
> And knows just how she got her!

On Julie's chart the teacher writes
"She's such a slow responder.
She'll never learn how fulcrums work,
The concept's just beyond her!"

Although it is generally enhanced by the use of cooperative learning, the learning cycle can be incorporated into most teaching situations with little modification of classroom arrangement or materials. It primarily involves an ideological shift in lesson presentation and teaching responsibility. The basic idea is to begin lessons by engaging students in hands-on exploration rather than giving them vocabulary lists, lectures, Power Point slide copies, or lists of rules. They then develop the lists and rules through careful teacher guidance.

The teacher holds up a standard piece of typing paper and tries to "fly" it across the room. The students giggle as the teacher makes several unsuccessful attempts to get the paper to move in a certain direction. Then the teacher distributes paper, scissors, and paper clips. Students are asked to do whatever they like to their papers in order to get them to travel the farthest distance across the room. The children design, fold, cut, compare, fly, modify, retry, discuss, and finally emerge with finished products ready for testing. During the exploration, student comments will reflect their experiences:

"Hey, his is going farther than mine. I'm going to fold my wings like that!"

"Look, if you get rid of some of the extra paper, it will stay in the air longer."

"I'm making my wings pointed because I've never seen an airplane that wasn't pointed!"

The teacher is using the first stage of the learning cycle to engage students in solving a problem that requires them to use process skills to gather and organize data. The teacher closely monitors the group and guides them through open-ended questions addressed to individuals and groups:

"Do you think there's a reason that airplanes have pointed noses? What could it be?"

"Why do you think folding the wings makes the plane go farther than leaving them flat?"

"Is there anything else that flies that is modeled like this?"

In this example, the science teacher is using an exploratory activity that allows all students to encounter the same experience at the same time, giving them an equal starting point from which to construct their learning. By encouraging students to become active participants in their own learning, the teacher's role changes from *teller of facts* to *facilitator of discovery*. By first asking students to use their prior knowledge to construct a product, the teacher has engaged them in learning through an activity that arouses their interest and allows for exploration, discovery, questioning, and discussion (Silver, 1998).

As the students continue to explore, they discover that certain laws of aerodynamics seem to apply to all of their creations. They begin to articulate what they have observed in their own words. The teacher helps them relate their terms in their explanations (*falls down* or *the harder you throw it*) to the vocabulary she wants to introduce (*the pull of gravity* and *thrust*). Next, he or she may show a computer model of flight along with appropriate dialogue to help develop the concepts and clarify the explanations. Because the students have had a shared concrete experience, they are ready to participate in scientific discussions about *lift, yaw, thrust, drag,* and *gravity.* They are able to compare their observations from the data they collected in the previous explorations.

Once the students demonstrate an understanding of how actual flight occurs, the teacher asks them to apply what they have learned to pictures or computerized versions of cartoons involving flight. Learners are asked to state whether or not they believe the cartoon characters and contraptions could really fly, and to give rational explanations for their hypotheses. Students can be asked to circle the areas of discrepancy and indicate how they believe this might be remedied.

The children are actively involved in learning as they use their newly acquired skills and understandings to construct deeper meanings and broader applications of their discoveries. The teacher has carefully guided the students through the three phases of the learning cycle and can be assured that students have developed their own concepts and can apply them to new situations.

 *A Note About the Learning Cycle*

The learning cycle has been described in similar forms with three to six steps of varying names. For the purpose of this chapter, I have used a model first presented to me in 1987 at an NSF-sponsored Operations Physics Training Program in San Diego, CA. The model has its roots in the Science Curriculum Improvement Study (SCIS), an NSF-sponsored elementary science program developed in the 1960s.

The Learning Cycle's Three Phases

Teachers and students using the learning cycle move through a series of phases or steps as they develop new concepts. The learning cycle is never a one-way progression. At any point in a lesson, learners may shift back and forth among the phases. It is the teacher's responsibility to monitor and informally assess where the students are, and where they need to go next.

Exploration Phase

The exploration phase initiates students' interaction with information, materials, and each other in order to investigate an open-ended question. All class members are given common, concrete experiences that challenge them to gather and organize data and compare their answers. Lessons involving paradoxical or conflicting information capitalize on their natural curiosity.

Often the exploration phase of the learning cycle is launched with a situation or question designed to capture the interest of students. A problem can be posed in which new information that is introduced is inconsistent with knowledge previously thought to be true (i.e., the teacher cannot just fly a flat piece of paper across the room). During this motivational phase students are encouraged to manipulate materials and explore ideas without specific outcomes designated by the teacher. Students use their skills to gather and organize data.

Most learning cycle advocates suggest that teachers use classroom activities to make sure that all students share the same experience. Students who have not achieved proficiency in English, who are main-streamed into classes, or who have not had the same experiential background as their peers can find themselves at a disadvantage for learning in a traditional setting. The exploration phase helps build a common ground for all. Some subjects more easily lend themselves to active classroom activities than others, but no matter what the subject, it is imperative that the lesson starts from a point shared by all.

Many teachers find that they can use a collective past experience (being scared at night, visiting a relative, eating a favorite food, solving a mystery) to illustrate a concept or begin a discussion. My advice regarding drawing on common experiences is to be sure that they are indeed shared by each student.

In the early 70s I was teaching middle grade students in an extremely rural community. We were all delighted when the first "local" mall was built in the closest big city, which was about a 50-minute drive away. Several months after the mall had opened, I decided to create a little enthusiasm for a writing assignment by having students write about a remembered trip to the mall. I asked my students to raise their hands if they had visited the mall. All hands went up.

I put the students into groups and asked them to come up with a list of descriptive words to describe their mall experience. The activity was a major flop. Irritable students snapped at each other, disagreed, and generally botched the assignment. I did not know why.

That spring I figured it out when we took our students to the city on a field trip. We made a stop at the mall. A group of girls followed me into a large department store, and as we were standing there getting our bearings, one of the young ladies nudged me and asked, "Ms. Silver, how much does it cost to ride the ride?"

I had no idea what she was talking about. "What ride?" I asked. She pointed to the escalator. Then it dawned on me—she had never been to a mall in her life. I wondered how many of my children had told me a fib in order to protect their esteem among their peers.

Since that time, I have become cautious about assuming anything regarding my students' experiences. I find it better for all concerned if I can provide the introductory activity in the classroom.

Concept Development Phase

The concept development phase builds on student curiosity, discoveries, and inquiries as the teacher helps students to organize the data they have collected. At this point, teachers clarify terms and concepts that have been developed. In this phase, students are far more receptive to vocabulary lists, direct instruction, and investigating other resources because their earlier explorations have shown them the relevance of the lesson. They also are far more likely to retain ideas and concepts because they begin to see patterns and connections to their knowledge of the world. The concept development phase is, and has always been, a time for the teacher to provide this direct instruction if needed.

It is an excellent time for teachers to use multi-sensory and multi-task choices for students to learn by capitalizing on their own strength areas. Students are involved as they are guided to create explanations, classifications, or hypotheses through discussions, mini-lectures, research, models, and so forth.

With the advent of the Internet, learners are literally linked to any of the best research, models, and examples they would like to explore. The key idea in the learning cycle is that although this phase has traditionally been used to introduce lessons, research tells us that it is better placed after the exploration phase. This phase is greatly enhanced by the teacher's ability to utilize effective questioning techniques.

Concept Application Phase

During the concept application phase, teachers challenge students to apply their knowledge to real-world situations and to explore broader applications of their discoveries. The teacher can pose new situations and questions to ensure deeper understanding.

Authentic assessment falls naturally into the concept application phase. According to Newmann, Marks, & Gamoran (1995), assessment strategies are moving beyond superficial levels of comprehension and towards deeper understandings such as:

- construction of knowledge
  Students should construct or produce knowledge, instead of merely reproducing or identifying understandings that others have created.

- disciplined inquiry
  Students should engage in cognitive work that requires them to rely on a field of knowledge, search for understanding, and communicate their ideas and findings in elaborate forms.

- value beyond school
  Students' accomplishments should have value—either aesthetic, utilitarian, or personal—beyond just documenting their competence.

If educators truly want students to become autonomous, lifelong learners, shouldn't they assess that which they say they truly value even though it is indeed harder to measure?

A Note About Concept Application

It is certainly more difficult to create divergent tasks that compel students to apply concepts to a broader perspective. Teachers who are firmly grounded in their subject areas, and who are not afraid themselves to think outside the lines, will foster within their students a spirit of wonder and delight in learning.

Several examples of lessons taught in the learning cycle format follow:

EXAMPLE 1: MATH CLASS

Students are asked to count the number of squares in the picture.

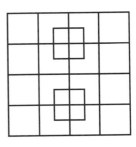

Answers vary from 27–40. The teacher looks at the class uncertainly, then places a transparency of the squares on the overhead projector and begins to count the obvious squares (the 1 big one, the 18 small ones, and the 8 tiny ones in the middle) and says, "See? There are just 27."

Outraged students point out the teacher forgot to count squares formed by the 2 x 2 small squares. The teacher agrees they are correct and counts 9 additional squares. "You are right! There are actually 36 squares."

A few very observant students tell the teacher that she has forgotten to count the 4 squares formed by the 3 x 3 small squares. "Well, I'll be. You are right again! There are 4 of those, and that makes 40 in all!"

The teacher then asks, "When I asked you to count the squares, what were you looking for?" Students reply, "Something that has 4 sides."

The teacher draws a 4-sided object with curved lines. The students say, "No, the 4 sides have to be straight."

The teacher draws a rectangle. The students say, "No, the 4 sides have to be straight and equal."

The teacher draws a rhombus. The students again modify their definition to include a right angle.

The teacher sums it up, "Okay, a square has to have 4 straight equal sides and a 90° angle, is that correct?"

Because the **students** are the ones who generated the definition, they are far more likely to remember it. For an assessment, the teacher passes out sheets with all kinds of polygons drawn on it. She asks the students to tell her whether or not each polygon is a square and tell her why. She then challenges students to create a piece of artwork using only squares.

EXAMPLE 2: LANGUAGE ARTS CLASS

After students have mastered the concept of nouns, verbs, and adjectives, the teacher hands groups of students a copy of a story from a popular teen magazine. She asks students to compile a list of all the words ending in -ly. She tells them to group the -ly words according to their functions in the sentences. Then she asks students to look for any emerging patterns they detect and be ready to report them to the entire group.

Students point out that most of their -ly words are used to fine-tune other words, which are verbs, adjectives, and other words. The teacher then introduces the term **adverb** and asks the students if they can come up with a general rule about -ly words. They tell her that words ending in -ly are adverbs.

She writes the following phrases on the board:

she sang brilliantly	a scholarly report
he cried long and hard	driving exceedingly fast
a lovely flower	he surely knew the answers
she wants it done now	a truly beautiful sunset
their progress was painstakingly slow	a tiny fly

Students are asked to test their hypothesis about all -ly words being adverbs. Through thoughtful, probing questions, the teacher helps students discover that not all words ending in -ly are adverbs, and words which act as adverbs do not all end in -ly.

The teacher then asks students to create a poem, an advertisement, a song, a rap, or a short paragraph that contains at least 15 adverbs used correctly.

EXAMPLE 3: SOCIAL STUDIES CLASS

The teacher gives each group of students a fictitious land map. The map key helps students locate water sources, mountains, fertile soil, desert areas, trees, caves, and natural resources. It shows average temperature and rainfall for each region. Each group is to pretend that they are early settlers and decide where they will establish their town. A representative from each group presents their group's location plans and tells why they made their selection.

The teacher then guides the students in recognizing the similar selections and reasons among all groups.

The teacher then gives students a map of the towns actually established by early settlers moving west. They compare the early town locations with the criteria established in their introductory activity. Students read in their history books about the westward movement, do a Web quest study, or find other ways to research the content knowledge.

For an assessment, students are asked to pick any major city in the United States and discuss what factors initially contributed to its location.

Effective Questioning

Questioning is an often overlooked strategic teaching tool. Effective questioning techniques can help teachers discover student experiences, understandings, and misconceptions. Questioning can also help guide student thinking and learning.

Questions can generally be regarded as being in one of three learning cycle phases or levels:

First Level:
Exploration Phase

Students are asked to gather or recall information.

Second Level:
Concept Development Phase

Students are asked to analyze, classify, compare, contrast, distinguish, explain, group, infer, make an analogy, organize, or synthesize.

Third Level:
Concept Application Phase

Students are encouraged to think intuitively, creatively, and hypothetically. They may be called on to apply a principle, build a model, evaluate, extrapolate, forecast, generalize, hypothesize, imagine, judge, predict, or speculate.

It is important to think carefully about what kinds of questions to ask students before teaching a lesson. Experienced teachers and certainly novice teachers will want to write out questions they want to ask when they teach the lesson. Giving thought to the kinds of questions that will be asked can help a teacher think about the aim of the lesson, and what it is students should know and be able to do when they leave class. Even hands-on, active-learning experiences are not complete without a follow-up opportunity for students to clarify what they learned and extend their learning to new and novel situations. The questions posed cue students to the level of thinking expected of them.

Technique Tips for Effective Questioning

- Always ask the question before calling on a student. Calling an individual student's name before the question is asked signals to the other students that they don't have to think about it.

- Avoid bombarding students with too much teacher talk. Strive to talk less and listen more.

- Wait time should be more than two seconds, and can be as long as six seconds. Practice to get comfortable with this technique.

    Because of my Type-A personality, this was really hard for me. I used to hand a designated student—usually one who needed help to stay focused—a timer and ask her or him to help me in gauging my wait time.

- Practice calling on ALL students. (It's harder than it seems!) Consider drawing names randomly, marking names on a seating chart as they are called, or creating another way to ensure that all students are given a chance to answer at some point during the lesson. DO NOT let a few students monopolize the question-answer session.

- Give the same think time to all students! Often teachers give the perceived brighter students more time to generate an answer than those who are thought to be not so bright.

- Require students to wait to be called on. This helps ensure that students are called on evenly and fairly. It also helps students who need help in controlling impulsivity.

- It is motivating and cognitively helpful to have other students respond to or elaborate on an answer rather than always having the teacher react to each individual answer.

- Ask students to metacognate (orally describe their thinking process) about how they got their answers. This is a great help to students who need tips on how to make certain connections, and it promotes higher-order thinking.

- When giving a follow-up comment, use strong praise sparingly. It is more beneficial to have students comment on each other's answers.

- Avoid bluffing an answer to a student question for which you do not have an answer. Be a good model in problem solving to find it.

- Encourage students to ask questions about process as well as content.

(adapted from Kellough and Kellough, Secondary School Teaching: A Guide to Methods and Resources, Planning for Competence, 1999.)

Drumming to the Beat of Different Marchers

Why the Learning Cycle Works

Instructional specialists advocate this kind of student-centered, active learning because it gives learners tasks that relate to their concerns, allows them to pursue their own interests, offers links to the outside world, and stimulates curiosity by introducing unexpected or unique information.

Research shows that learning is dependent on these factors:

- the student's motivation
- the student's active involvement in the experience of learning
- linking the new concepts with familiar information
- being able to take new information and apply it to the real world

Redesigning Lessons to Incorporate the Learning Cycle

 It's not so much that we're afraid of change
or so in love with the old ways,
but it's that place in-between that we fear.
It's like being between trapezes. It's Linus when his
blanket is in the dryer. There's nothing to hold on to.

— Marilyn Ferguson, The Aquarian Conspiracy

Redesigning an instructional and assessment strategy to incorporate the learning cycle is well worth the effort. However, it does take time and considerable thought. Many of the curriculum resources and textbooks currently used are already based on this model. Try using a computer search engine to get ideas. Enter the concept to be taught, the age of the students, and the parameter words "learning cycle." Try this out using Google Search. Enter *math integers, elementary,* and *learning cycle.*

Some subjects are easier to adapt to this model than others. Whatever the case, take the time to give serious thought about how to ensure that all students will have a reasonable chance to progress towards the intended outcomes. Do not try to redesign all class lessons at one time.

First, redo lessons that easily lend themselves to this model. Then, over time try to change the majority of what is taught to incorporate at least some aspects of the learning cycle. Constantly reflect on what is working and what is not. Keep the things that are, and change the things that are not.

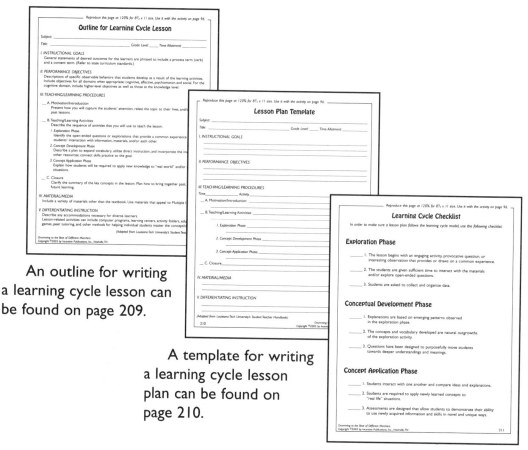

An outline for writing a learning cycle lesson can be found on page 209.

A template for writing a learning cycle lesson plan can be found on page 210.

Use these along with the learning cycle checklist on page 211 to facilitate planning.

Tips for
Instituting Reform Practices in Your Classroom

- Don't try to do it all at once. Start with one idea, then try another.

- Don't try to do it alone. Involve other teachers, parents, and administrators.

- Get involved in professional networking, especially through subject area organizations. Read their journals, attend their workshops, subscribe to their newsletters, and visit their recommended sites on the Internet.

- Use the Internet to find new ideas, talk with other teachers, and ask questions.

- Talk with others about the changes being made. Let parents, students, and other teachers know what is happening.

- Communicate with business and industry for practical ideas about real-life assessment practices.

- Enjoy the process. Reflect on successes as well as failures.

Adapted from the
1991 National Council for Teachers of Math (NCTM) booklet
Mathematics Assessment: Myths, Models,
Good Questions, and Practical Suggestion

Summary

In his book, *Awakening Genius in the Classroom,* Thomas Armstrong (1998) strongly advocates models that promote a natural rhythm to learning. He is concerned about tapping the source of what drives the learning process in every child. The learning cycle seems to be a good fit with his 12 aspects of students' intrinsic motivation to learn—curiosity, playfulness, imagination, joy, wonder, creativity, wisdom, inventiveness, vitality, sensitivity, flexibility, and humor.

In summary, it can be said that teaching for understanding requires different strategies than those traditionally used for instruction. In a lesson designed to meet the needs of many marchers, students' misconceptions are addressed through exploration and discussion. Students explore their own questions as a way of acquiring new knowledge.

In the educational community, there is agreement that traditional direct teaching is not the most effective way to promote conceptual change or real understanding of new concepts. It is generally agreed that a constructivist approach like the learning cycle is more suited to individualizing instruction and thus, more successfully meets the needs of all learners in terms of student motivation, understanding, and development of higher level thinking skills.

Recommended Reading List

Hollas, Betty. *Differentiating Instruction in a Whole-Group Setting.*
　　Peterborough, NH: Crystal Springs Books, 2005.

Jackson, Anthony W., and Gayle A. Davis. *Turning Points 2000:*
　　Educating Adolescents in the 21st Century. NY: Teachers College
　　Press, 2000.

Johnson, Doug. *The Indispensable Teacher's Guide to Computer Skills.*
　　Worthington, OH: Linworth Publishing, 2002.

Tomlinson, Carol A. *The Differentiated Classroom: Responding to the*
　　Needs of All Learners. Alexandria, VA: Association for Supervision
　　and Curriculum Development (ASCD), 1999.

Wiggins, Grant, and Jay McTighe. *Understanding by Design.* Alexandria,
　　VA: Association for Supervision and Curriculum Development
　　(ASCD), 1998.

Wormeli, Rick. *Summarization in Any Subject: 50 Techniques to Improve*
　　Student Learning. Alexandra, VA: ASCD, 2005.

Chapter 5

Multiple Intelligences

and

Different Learning Styles

If They All Have Gifts,
Why Don't They Open Them?

A Debate

The Inclusive Teacher vs. *The Exclusive Teacher*

I help them learn how they are smart.
I test how slow they are.
I like it if their ways depart.
I just want what is par.

I try to differentiate.
I give them all one task.
My role is to accommodate.
They ought to do what's asked.

Effective teaching is my creed
We get through every text.
I give them all the time they need
Slow learners have me vexed.

I must address each learning style.
I show them one right way.
Exciting methods get a trial.
I don't have time to play!

Alternative assessment's great.
I only need one test.
With students I collaborate.
Goal setting I detest!

Assignments are not uniform.
We're all on the same page.
My teaching methods show reform.
I don't "improve with age!"

I want to get them in "the flow."
I wish they understood . . .
So they'll have fun with what they know.
I'd teach them if I could.

Which teacher
would you like to emulate?

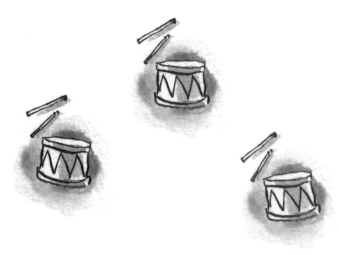

From My Experience

I am often asked if I support the gifted education program. My response has always been that I think the gifted curriculum is exceptional and definitely should be available—to everyone. It is my belief that all children really do have gifts. I think that it is the responsibility of educators to *go in after* vastly different students—armed with best practices and with educational plans customized to meet their specific needs.

One way that we can tap more of the gifts in students is to provide them with divergent opportunities for success. Recent research in multiple intelligences (MI) and learning styles strengthens the call for varied teaching strategies and assessment. My favorite educational maxim for the decade comes from Howard Gardner, MI researcher, who popularized the notion, "It's not about how smart they are, it's about **how** they are smart."

All students have abilities, but in our naïve belief that some strengths and learning styles are more valuable than others, we have excluded many learners from feeling capable and from being successful. Students who don't learn it *the right way* are told that they will have to do it again and try harder next time.

Remediation in this traditional sense is a bit ridiculous. If a student cannot correctly do the first 25 problem sets, why assign 25 more of the exact same thing? Why not try something entirely different? I much prefer the idea of *compensation,* which is helping students learn to use their strengths to work around the areas in which they are struggling. Most teachers truly want to include all students, but they are often unsure how to do it.

Sometimes I am such a hypocrite. I constantly tell adults to listen carefully to the voice within each child, yet I failed to do exactly that when my youngest stepson, Andy, told me that he wanted to be a musician.

Andy's Story

Andy had never had a music lesson, been in band, or even played an instrument (unless you count spoons, pencils, and any other utensils that could be commandeered for an impromptu percussion performance).

Being a seasoned middle school teacher, I am very familiar with the drummings and tappings of adolescent boys. I ignored Andy and hoped that he would "grow out of it." One day, he asked me if I would help talk his dad into buying him a set of snare drums.

I vividly remember my warm and caring reply, "Now let me see if I have this straight, Andy. We have five boys, four of whom are teenagers, and your thinking is that what we are missing in this house is a set of SNARE DRUMS! I don't think so!"

Undaunted, young Mr. Silver got a job and earned enough money to buy the drums himself. Very soon after he began playing real drums it became obvious that not only did he have a musical intelligence, but also he was musically gifted. He had told all of the adults in his life this fact for years, but none of us had paid any attention to him.

Now here's the amazing part. Before Andy came to live with his dad and me in the eighth grade, he had been tested and labeled as a slow, low-level learner. Previous educators told his parents that the prognosis for his success was not good because he was such a poor reader. One teacher had even commented that Andy would probably never graduate from high school.

When we enrolled him in the local school where my other sons attended, we were informed that his records indicated a need for special classes. The label a group of educators had so easily placed on him when he was in the second grade deeply disturbed me. In spending time with Andy, I realized that he was an extremely perceptive, uncommonly deep thinker. We wanted him put in regular education classes with his peers at his new school. The administrators balked, but because I know the law and how the system works, I was able to get Andy placed where we wanted him. Despite his very low standardized test scores and his documented learning disabilities (dyslexia, among others) he was placed in regular classes with his peers. I felt temporarily vindicated, until a thought hit me: What happens to the children who have no advocate? What becomes of students who start believing the labels put on them?

Even being placed in regular classes in a new school with a new start was not a simple solution for Andy. Years of being both overtly and covertly told that he was not as promising as the others had taken its toll on him. He had lost his spirit for trying because it was so hard for him to learn in an R^3 (read, recite, regurgitate) world. In the few classes he had that teachers actually let him do something (rather than just read from the text and answer questions), he did fairly well. In classes where teachers encouraged passionate debates about interesting issues, Andy soared. But classes such as those were the exception, and most of the time he was required to listen, take notes, memorize, and write about what he remembered being told. He really tried, but he told me he just could not get the information to stick.

It was the music that turned things around for our young percussionist/learner. When he began playing in earnest, he would study while tapping out rhythms. The long passages of narrative that Andy struggled to remember came easily to him when he attached the desired information to the drum riffs he would later play back in his head during class. He used his musical ability to remember facts and important data. It worked! (How many of us still sing the "A-B-C Song" in our heads when filing papers?) The more success he had in school, the harder he tried. He eventually taught himself to use his music as a compensatory study skill to help him remember all kinds of things. This kid who was "never going to graduate from high school" ended up graduating on time, with his class, and with honors! At the graduation ceremony, his mom leaned over and thanked me. I quickly pointed out that I appreciated her sentiment, but it was Andy who was the one responsible for his success. He had found his own voice, his own step, his own rhythm. I just drummed along

After this "slow, low-level learner" was awarded the John Phillips Sousa Music Award his senior year, he went to college on a music scholarship, studied to be an astro-geologist (okay, a rock star), and finished college on the dean's list with a degree in jazz performance and a certification to teach. Andy is now a successful musician in Austin, Texas, who teaches part-time and loves his life.

Andy actually helped crystallize for me what I had known intuitively for quite a while. Sometimes students who have difficulty memorizing large chunks of narrative can easily recall information that is put to a beat or a melody. Many teachers were creating raps, patters, and songs to help reinforce tedious information long before multiple intelligence proponents came along to tell us why it worked.

One teacher I know had her high school biology students make up a musical square dance that demonstrated how cells divide. They sang and danced their way through the process of mitosis with relative ease, and I doubt one of them will ever forget the names of the organelles or the sequence of the phases.

To learn more about the power of attaching new learning to music, read Don Campbell's *The Mozart Effect*.

But musical intelligence is just one of the ways that students can be smart. There are at least seven others. Effective teachers have been using a kind of multiple intelligence lesson design for years when they let students act out the molecules or create a mural of a historical timeline or present a first person oral book report. Good teachers have always found ways to honor student abilities and incorporate them into effective instruction and assessment.

The good news is that educators today don't have to start from scratch. A myriad of information is available about how to integrate multiple intelligences into lessons through our professional journals, the Internet, and in-service training. Scores of books and Web sites with lesson plans for teaching and assessing with multiple intelligences are now available. Beware of blindly adopting a prepackaged lesson design and missing the depth of what Howard Gardner first described. The point of multiple intelligences is to assist teachers in creating the best learning experiences possible for each student. It is a very individual process that cannot be duplicated mechanically.

Multiple intelligences theories are being discussed and used in ever-widening educational circles. A cornerstone to the principle that "no child will be left behind" is the premise that students' intelligences will be identified (They all have strengths in at least one or two areas!) and used to maximize their understandings of the world around them. Helping them learn to capitalize on their competencies is a key way of inspiring them to be lifelong learners. Researchers are finding more and more that when students are taught and assessed using their strongest areas for even a small part of the school day, their overall learning and performance is enhanced.

Howard Gardner's Multiple Intelligences

Howard Gardner first described seven intelligences in his 1983 book, *Frames of Mind*. He said then that his research findings represented his "best-faith effort" to identify intelligence less as a single entity and more as a multi-dimensional model that can be identified through empirical findings dealing with neurobiology, cultural history, and cognitive psychology. He acknowledged then that no empirically-based theory is ever established permanently and said that his theory would be revised if new findings from the laboratory and from the field emerged. True to his word, Gardner added an eighth intelligence to his list in 1995.

Gardner did not write his Multiple Intelligences Theory with an educational end in mind. He has often commented that he is as surprised as anyone at how quickly the education community embraced his findings. He has urged users of his theory to adhere to three tenets (1995):

   1) Cultivate skills that are valued in the community and society.

   2) Approach new concepts and subjects in a variety of ways.

   3) Personalize instruction as much as possible.

Gardner believes that the best use of his research findings is for teachers to recognize students' individual ways of being smart. He urges teachers to help students use their distinct combinations of intelligences to be successful in school and in life. Checkley (1997) offers this summary of the eight intelligences:

SUMMARY OF GARDNER'S EIGHT INTELLIGENCES

Linguistic intelligence	Linguistic intelligence is the capacity to use language (your native language, and perhaps other languages) to express what is on your mind and to understand other people. Poets really specialize in linguistic intelligence, but any kind of writer, orator, speaker, lawyer, or a person for whom language is an important stock in trade highlights linguistic intelligence.
Logical-mathematical intelligence	People with a highly developed logical-mathematical intelligence understand the underlying principles of some kind of a causal system, the way a scientist or a logician does; or can manipulate numbers, quantities, and operations, the way a mathematician does.

Spatial intelligence	Spatial intelligence refers to the ability to represent the spatial world internally in your mind—the way a sailor or airplane pilot navigates the large spatial world, or the way a chess player or sculptor represents a more circumscribed spatial world. Spatial intelligence can be used in the arts or in the sciences. A learner who is spatially intelligent and oriented toward the arts, is more likely to become a painter or sculptor or an architect than, say, a musician or a writer. Similarly, certain sciences like anatomy or topology emphasize spatial intelligence.
Bodily kinesthetic intelligence	Bodily kinesthetic intelligence is the capacity to use the whole body or parts of the body—hand, fingers, and arms—to solve a problem, make something, or put on some kind of a production. The most evident examples are people in athletics or the performing arts, particularly dance or acting.
Musical intelligence	Musical intelligence is the capacity to think in music, to be able to hear patterns, recognize them, remember them, and perhaps manipulate them. People who have a strong musical intelligence don't just remember music easily—they can't get it out of their minds because it's so omnipresent. *Now, some people will say, "Yes, music is important, but it's a talent." And I say, "Fine, let's call it a talent." But then we have to leave the word intelligent out of all discussions of human abilities.*
Interpersonal intelligence	Interpersonal intelligence is understanding other people. It's an ability we all need, but is very important to teachers, clinicians, salespersons, or politicians. Anybody who deals with other people has to be skilled in the interpersonal sphere.
Intra-personal intelligence	Intra-personal intelligence refers to having an understanding of oneself, what one can do, what one wants to do, how one reacts to things, which things to avoid, and which things to gravitate toward. People who have a good understanding of themselves attract others because people with intra-personal intelligences tend not to make mistakes. They tend to know what they can do. They tend to know what they can't do. And they tend to know where to go if they need help.
Naturalist intelligence	Naturalist intelligence designates the human ability to discriminate among living things (plants, animals), as well as sensitivity to other features of the natural world (clouds, rock configurations). This ability was clearly of value in man's evolutionary past to hunters, gatherers, and farmers. It continues to be central in such roles as botanist or chef. *I also speculate that much of our consumer society exploits the naturalist intelligences, which can be mobilized in the discrimination among cars, sneakers, kinds of makeup, and the like.*

Introducing Students to Multiple Intelligences

Students like to construct their own intelligence profiles using various inventories. An in-depth consideration of their major strength areas is a valuable metacognitive tool for students. There are several multiple intelligences inventories available in current literature as well as on the Internet.

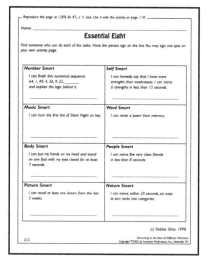

Use an icebreaker activity to introduce students to the idea of multiple intelligences. An example of one is found on page 212. The purpose of the activity is to encourage learners to think about the different areas of intelligence. Participants are to mix freely and get different people to sign the blanks. Each participant may sign his or her own sheet once. In order to record a name in the blank, the person signing must actually perform the task (not just say that she or he can do it).

After the activity is completed, ask students if some of the tasks are more appealing to them than others. Students always answer in the affirmative. Explain to them that research has now alerted educators to the fact that everyone is smart in at least one or two of the eight intelligences, and no one is inordinately smart in all eight.

To illustrate this, explain to them about idiot savants who show dramatic abilities in one area and very little ability in others. Most of them have seen the movie *Rain Man*, so they have a visual image of how this can occur. Tell them that to a less extraordinary degree, all humans are more highly advanced in one or two intelligences than in the others.

While everyone has some quantity of every intelligence, certain areas will be intrinsically easier for them. All students have a unique blend of ranges and combinations of the eight intelligences. Given that an individual can improve every intelligence area with effort, everyone should work to improve the areas where she or he is not so strong while capitalizing on the areas that are strong.

To help them ascertain their individual strength areas, give them one of the many intelligence profiles available to fill out. Profiles are beneficial in helping students discover the areas where they are smart. (If the term *intelligence* is troubling, think of intelligences as areas of strength, areas in which the student demonstrates a pre-dispositional leaning, or groups of tasks which seem to come easily for the student.)

Using Multiple Intelligences to Assess Students

Inventory checklists can be used to determine strengths and help individuals understand their own potential. Teachers will find checklists useful for making observations about students. It is helpful for educators to get a sense about the strengths of each child in order to help design appropriate instructional and assessment strategies.

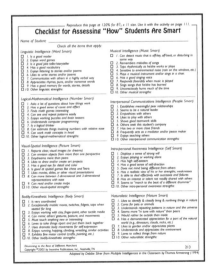

No one is advocating that every concept be taught in eight different ways, but the point is to realize that any important topic can be and probably should be taught in more than one way. One teacher checklist can be found on page 213.

Howard Gardner maintains that learning is a consequence of thinking—and good thinking is learnable by all students. He believes that learning should include deep understanding, which involves the flexible, active use of knowledge. Gardner contends that students should both receive instruction using multiple intelligence strategies, and, just as importantly, be assessed using the same strategies.

Undertaking alternative assessment takes creativity, thoughtful planning, and time. As with all new approaches, teachers should start with incremental steps and proceed at a comfortable pace. Doing something innovative occasionally takes a little public relations groundwork with students, colleagues, administrators, and parents. Ask them to withhold judgment until plans are fully implemented. Be ready to coach them through the process and listen attentively to their apprehensions. It is important that teachers ask for patience. Eventually, most concerns will be assuaged. It is hard to argue with success, and customizing teaching to fit selected outcomes will eventually lead to enhanced learning for all students.

There are literally hundreds of books and resources available to educators who wish to find ideas for developing inventive ways that allow students to demonstrate their genuine understandings.

My best advice is to use prepackaged programs only as guides. Generally, teachers should adapt the work of others to fit their exact needs. Give deep thought to what essential ideas and skills students will be taught to master.

Many teachers brainstorm with students about how best to find out what they understand. They let the students help develop the standards and expectations for demonstrating their knowledge of a desired concept as well as the rubric that will determine their progress towards the goal. Finally, educators should seek to give students options about how they will show what they know and can do. Not every assessment has to be designed to give students eight different ways of demonstrating success, but at least occasionally students need to have choices other than traditional paper and pencil. On the next page are just a few ideas for starters.

Different Ways to Find Out What Students Understand

- Present a news report
- Write and perform a rap
- Make a chart or diagram
- Create an invention
- Teach someone else
- Write a letter to the editor
- Conduct a discussion
- Create an advertisement
- Write an essay
- Participate in a simulation
- Create a poem
- Produce a photo essay
- Write an analogy
- Participate in a mock trial
- Design and teach a class
- Devise a new recipe
- Write a monologue
- Illustrate a math concept
- Critique a book
- Complete a demonstration
- Make a scrapbook
- Participate in a debate
- Make an editorial video
- Design a structure
- Develop a collection
- Design a game
- Judge an event

- Write a diary from someone else's perspective
- Produce a multimedia presentation
- Conduct an interview
- Design a Web Quest
- Create a puppet show
- Create cartoons
- Create a flow chart
- Give a performance
- Defend a theory
- Create a brochure
- Develop an exhibit
- Create a dance
- Keep a journal log
- Create a report
- Make a plan
- Make a mural
- Create a new product
- Conduct an experiment
- Make a model
- Develop a rubric
- Write a book
- Make a learning center
- Draw a blueprint
- Perform a self-assessment
- Solve a mystery
- Conduct a Gallery Walk (Carousel Walk)
- Set up a system of checks and balances

Multiple Intelligence Theory has done much to advance the argument for differentiated instruction. No thinking person can acknowledge that children have unique blends of the eight intelligences and then advocate that they all be taught the same thing at the same time in the same way. Along that line educators should concentrate on finding valid ways that are not entirely based on literacy skills for assessing what students know.

Howard Gardner has stated repeatedly that he does not think his identified levels of intelligence should be used to label or sort remedial students. The knowledge that students are smart in different ways should empower teachers to seek optimum opportunities for each child's learning. The self-knowledge *that they are smart, too* encourages students to feel competent and to become successful learners.

An Introduction to Learning Styles

Another strong argument for differentiated instruction comes from the field of psychology. Behavioral and cognitive psychologists have long maintained that students come to school with certain inherent learning styles, many of which are at absolute odds with traditional teaching methods.

Before educators knew about multiple intelligences, teachers were encouraged by researchers to be mindful that students have fixed ways of internalizing new information. Educators were told that not all students learned equally well with traditional teaching strategies.

I am embarrassed to admit it, but I was in my thirties before I discovered a very important lesson about my "outside-the-lines" teaching style. For years I had the condescending belief that if everyone would just "chill out" and approach life with the same spontaneous light-hearted attitude I had, the world would be a better place.

I patiently tried to deal with my very best friend (a teacher, of course) who made lists of her lists and organized her life with all the passion of a tax auditor. She often became frustrated with my attempts to skip her planned meetings (I would rather tie rattlesnakes in knots than go to a meeting!) and was frequently impatient with my lack of preparation and disregard for details. Likewise I was regularly put off by her need to address every possible contingency with a "back-up plan," and laughed about her calendar that looked like a strategic military plan. Basically, I balked at her attempts to control me, and she cringed at what she saw as my flightiness and irresponsibility.

In my classroom, I had similar difficulties with students who wanted to know exactly what, when, and how I was going to teach. One student came to my sixth grade class on the first day of school and wanted a syllabus of what we'd be doing for the rest of the year! I was annoyed that she put me on the spot like that for something so entirely unnecessary. I knew this was going to be a long year.

It really used to bother me that after I spent extraordinary amounts of time and energy making a lesson fun and exciting, some child would ask, "Aren't we supposed to be doing our spelling words now?" I wanted to choke him!

It disturbed me that when I told students like that just to relax because I would make sure we got around to everything, they would still be uptight. It troubled me when students would ask, "Is this going to be on the test?" My answer that they should enjoy the learning and not worry about the test did not seem to soothe them at all. There was a definite rub between a few of my students and me that I attributed to their inability to trust me and just loosen up.

Then, as a part of a professional improvement program, my very best friend and I drove to the "Big City" to attend a conference on learning styles. I had never even heard of learning styles, but I'm always in need of "styling tips," so I jumped at the chance to go. The two of us were introduced to the presenter, Dr. Anthony Gregorc, who had all the participants take his Style Delineator™ (1982). The instrument had a bunch of words that we were to rate from 4 to 1, according to our personal thoughts and feelings. We used our scores to graph our tendencies for the way we handled the immediate demands on our lives. I peeked at my friend's graph and was not at all surprised to see that hers was the exact opposite of mine.

When Dr. Gregorc asked for a show of hands from the participants whose highest score was in the abstract random (AR) group, I proudly shot my arm up. My friend looked quite dejected as our instructor told everyone to look around at those who had their hands up because we were the ones who tended to be the most fun, spontaneous people in the room. I beamed as he explained that others generally liked to be around us because we are so colorful. I was ready for him to let the rest of the group know that they should all strive to be like us ARs when he added, "By the way, these folks have no concept of time, they are terrible with details, and they frustrate the heck out of those of you who are trying to plan important things."

I shrank in my chair as my friend looked over smugly and said under her breath, "You got that right, Doc!"

Dr. Gregorc went on to point out the strengths and the weaknesses of his four categories: abstract random, abstract sequential, concrete random, and concrete sequential. All four categories, not just mine, were balanced by strong positive features, as well as inherent limitations. He told us that the way people internalize information and approach problem solving is static and instinctive.

It was like an epiphany for me. I suddenly realized that when others would not cooperate and do it my way, it wasn't so much that they were trying to subvert me personally, but rather that they were trying to use practices with which they were the most comfortable. When learners complained that *they couldn't do it the way I showed them, it was more a matter of style than a matter of intelligence or compliance.*

I listened intently to what my new prophet said. I took notes, asked questions, and later did follow-up research on the topic of learning styles. It totally changed the way I was teaching. I realized that I had been utilizing only the instructional methods that I found appealing. Because I am very random and do not like extensive reading assignments, drill and practice, step-by-step methodology, or any kind of rigid strategies, I simply did not use them. Because I am so abstract in my thinking, I never saw the need to use a chalkboard, an overhead projector, outlines, or even class notes.

My frenzied and unpredictable teaching techniques were fine for my abstract random students, but I suddenly understood that those who were more sequential and concrete were getting left out. No wonder they had seemed so bothered and confused by my frantic pace. It was time to change some of my practices.

Since that significant day, I have done considerable research on the topic of learning styles. I found that the concept of four basic personality types has its roots in ancient history and philosophy.

Whatever classification system you use, there is demonstrable evidence that individual learners can best be taught through differentiated instructional strategies and assessments.

Teachers can most effectively engage each and every learner by adapting differentiated approaches.

Gregorc's Four Basic Learning Styles

A Note About Gregorc's Learning Styles

The following classifications are the property of Dr. Anthony Gregorc. They have emerged from his extensive research on the topic of learning styles. A full presentation of this material is available online.

The Abstract Random

The abstract random learner's (ARL's) approach to change is subject to emotions and level of interest. ALR's approach to life is idealistic, emotional, and always intense. This learner prefers an environment that is active and vibrant, allowing emotional and physical freedom. ALRs are distinguishable by their attention to human behavior and an extraordinary ability to sense and interpret feelings. An ARL prefers to receive information in an unstructured manner, and is therefore, comfortable in groups and with busy environments. An ARL tends to evaluate all experiences *as a whole* and sees the world in *black and white*.

The Concrete Sequential

The concrete sequential learner (CSL) is usually slow and hesitant about change. This learner's approach to life is realistic, patient, and conservative. A CSL prefers an environment that is ordered, quiet, and stable. A CSL has a finely-tuned ability to derive information through direct, hands-on experience. This person has an extraordinary development of the five senses and likes touchable concrete materials.

This student likes step-by-step directions when confronted with a new situation. A CSL does not like surprises and prefers to be in control of most situations. A CSL is the one learner who not only looks for directions, but follows them!

The Abstract Sequential

The abstract sequential learner (ASL) is indecisive about change. This person focuses on knowledge and facts; an ASL insists upon documentation before *buying into* new ideas. An ASL's approach to life is realistic, serious, logically intellectual, and determined. An ASL likes an environment that is mentally stimulating, but non-authoritative.

ASLs like to direct their own learning. These students have excellent decoding abilities in the areas of written, verbal, and image symbols. ASLs have a preference for presentations that are rational and have substance. An ASL pays attention to detail and usually prefers to work alone.

The Concrete Random

The concrete random learner (CRL) is open and amenable to change; this person is sometimes the instigator of change. A CRL's approach to life is inquisitive and independent. He or she likes an environment that is competitive and stimulus-rich. This person has an experimental attitude that is often accompanied by a trial-and-error approach to problem solving. A CRL gets the gist of ideas quickly and demonstrates the uncanny ability to make intuitive leaps in exploring unstructured problem-solving experiences. This person is often self-motivated and not interested in details.

What Does This Mean for Teachers?

Please do not think that I am suggesting that teachers must cover every concept in four different styles (or eight different intelligences or a combination of both). That would be impossible, as well as counterproductive. Part of the job as an educator is to prepare students for the real world, and quite frankly, in most cases, our learners will have to conform to the edicts of the real world rather than the other way around.

Rather, I suggest that by designing a variety of experiences for students as each unit is planned, teachers are more likely to appeal to their different marchers and re-engage them in the learning process. It is a matter of purposefully planning lessons that offer a range of ways to internalize new information. For most of us, it is easy to plan activities in keeping with our own styles. The challenge is to blend activities that capitalize on each of the styles. (If you work on a team with colleagues who have different learning styles, this job becomes much easier.) The key is variety in the ways that information is presented. Plan for how students will practice processing it and create opportunities for them to demonstrate what they know. Teachers must be diligent in giving each student a chance at using his or her own best resources. Use the following suggestions to help you include strategies that are appropriate for every learner.

Appropriate Instructional Strategies for Different Learners

Abstract Random Learner	Concrete Random Learner
• Role playing • Team games • Short reading assignments • Discussions • Videos • Peer tutoring • Group investigations • Active, busy environments	• Independent study projects • Learning games • Simulations • Optional reading assignments • Open-ended discussions • Divergent thinking activities • Unstructured exploration time • Mini-lectures • Activities on the Internet • Moderately active environments
Abstract Sequential Learner	Concrete Sequential Learner
• Extensive reading assignments • Lecture with time for reflection • Debate • Essays • Quiet, well-controlled environments • Finding information on the World Wide Web • Research-based lessons • Individual projects • Journaling • Inquiry-based activities • Logic Problems	• Step-by-step directions • Workbooks • Drill and practice • Lectures with demonstrations • Labeling drawings and models • Well-structured field trips • Color-coded study organizers • Logical sequencing • Focused, quiet environments

Just for Clarification

Some people are confused by the association between learning styles and multiple intelligences. In this book, *Multiple Intelligence Theory* refers to content matters, and learning style theory refers to matters of process. It is my belief that learning styles are a fixed mode of understanding primarily used to master new skills and concepts. I think that a person's learning style transcends all intelligence levels. There are those who argue about a relationship between multiple intelligences and learning styles. So far, I am not satisfied with attempts to connect them, and I don't think they have to be linked. What I do know is that students learn in unique ways, and it is to everyone's benefit if teachers are encouraged to vary techniques, strategies, assignments, and assessments so that all students have a reasonable chance at success.

 If a doctor, lawyer, or dentist had 40 people in his office at one time, all of whom had different needs, and some of whom didn't want to be there and were causing trouble, and the doctor, lawyer, dentist, without assistance, had to treat them all with professional excellence for nine months, then he might have some conception of the classroom teacher's job.

— Donald D. Quinn

Flow State

Sometimes when students are engaged in activities and assessments that are well-matched to their individual needs, a wonderful thing happens. They don't hear the bell ring, they don't want to leave class, and they carry their love for learning away from the classroom with them. This ideal state is called **flow** and is considered by many theorists and educators as the best possible learning state.

Last summer my stepson, Andy (the kid who was once told by a teacher that he was "not a strong enough reader to graduate from high school") called to ask me a question about Mihalyi Csikszentmihalyi's (pronounced "me-high chick-SENT-me-high") concept of flow. Andy was struggling through one of Csikszentmihalyi's books because he was interested in promoting a flow state in his music students. I was very impressed. Most of the time, I cannot even get my graduate students to tackle the manuscripts of this researcher, but on his own, Andy Silver was plodding through Csikszentmihalyi's theory so that he could improve his own teaching. What a teacher!

Based on over two decades of study, psychologist Mihalyi Csikszentmihalyi has coined the term *flow* to refer to a state of concentrated action and awareness. A popular expression of this condition is *being in the zone.* Research subjects describe flow as a state of being so engaged in an activity (e.g., running, writing, exploring, painting, dancing, performing, reading) that the senses of time, space, and outside stimuli are temporarily suspended.

Respondents report that when they are in this depth of concentration, they feel energized and euphoric. They liken the feeling to being carried by a current, everything moving smoothly without effort.
   Csikszentmihalyi calls it flow—others call it fun.

Education is not the filling of a bucket,
   but the lighting of a fire.

— W. B. Yeats

Lev Vygotsky (1980) defines this best possible set-up as one that is in the student's "zone of proximal development." The zone of proximal development is the distance between the student's present developmental level and the student's potential level of development (e.g., one that is reasonably attainable and yet just far enough beyond easy reach to sustain interest—somewhere between anxiety and boredom). Csikszentmihalyi agrees that when task requirements are high and personal skills are used to their fullest extent, learners are more likely to be absorbed in the process. Optimally, students become engaged, focused, and willing to keep pushing the limits of their abilities. Psychologists believe that when the learning experience gives this kind of intrinsic reward, students are far more likely to become self-propelled, self-motivated lifelong learners.

> *My own conviction is that lifelong learning is not inspired by "teaching to the test," lock-step curriculum, or any other way of merely "filling the bucket." Master educators closely match the interests and abilities of students to fulfilling cognitive tasks. Thus, teachers help students learn the joy of the learning process rather than merely complying with preordained results. These "fire-lighters" are able to motivate, invigorate, and empower students with activities so relevant and engaging that the learning process just seems to flow. The mastery comes from being able to provide students tasks that are challenging, but still obtainable.*

Promoting Flow in the Classroom

Csikszentmihalyi (1991) suggests basic guidelines for those who wish to promote flow in the classroom. Teachers should:

- Be sensitive to students' goals and desires; use this knowledge to choose and frame activities that provide meaningful challenges.

- Empower students to take control of their own learning by giving them freedom within the context of clearly articulated goals.

- Provide clear and immediate feedback to students about how they are doing without making them feel inadequate or self-conscious.

- Arrange for students to have appropriate time to focus and help limit distractions.

Intuitive teachers observe when flow occurs naturally (such as a lively debate, writing in a journal, creating a multimedia presentation, playing a game, making and/or listening to music, or fashioning an art project) and learn to create similar experiences to engage students. They constantly monitor student activities and help them shift up or down depending on the difficulty of the task.

While the state of flow is an optimal learning situation for students, it is not something that normally occurs without intentional design by the teacher and purposeful effort by the learners. Experienced teachers make students aware that flow is something that requires work and responsibility on their part. They remind students that it was through deliberate practice and effort that Tiger Woods learned to swing a golf club, Britney Spears accomplished vocal timing and dance moves, and J. K. Rowling mastered the rules for syntax. Some drill and practice is often needed to make certain steps or movements so automatic that they no longer require conscious thought. This state of automaticity is needed in order to move on to higher levels of performance. Students more readily accept the repetitious tedium of learning basic skills when they are artfully blended with opportunities to engage in affirming states of flow.

Educators must find their own flow states in order to stay energized, excited, and effective in their work. Some school systems remain strongly entrenched in finding ways to select, organize, and distribute knowledge (*filling the buckets*), even though teachers know that paying attention to motivational issues (*lighting the fires*) is a more effective way to truly impact student learning. In short, filling the bucket is not effective because the results quickly evaporate.

It is not an easy task, but the results of helping students open their gifts are permanent and add to the joy of learning for all involved. By validating and utilizing students' multiple intelligences and learning styles, teachers can be far more effective in achieving short-term and long-range educational goals with students.

> *Thank you, Andy, and all the teachers who are out there lighting fires and drumming to the beat of their different marchers.*

Recommended Reading List

Armstrong, Thomas. *Awakening Genius in the Classroom.* Alexandria, VA: Association for Supervision and Curriculum Development (ASCD), 1998.

Burke, Kay. *How to Assess Authentic Learning. 3rd edition.* Prentice Hall, 2000.

Campbell, Don. *The Mozart Effect: Tapping the Power of Music to Heal the Body, Strengthen the Mind, and Unlock the Creative Spirit.* NY: Harper Paperbacks, 2001.

Campbell, Linda and Bruce Campbell. *MIs and Student Achievement: Success Stories from Six Schools.* Alexandria, VA: Association for Supervision and Curriculum Development (ASCD), 1999.

Lazear, David G. *Eight Ways of Knowing. 3rd edition.* Thousand Oaks, CA: Corwin Press, 1998.

Tomlinson, Carol Ann. *How to Differentiate Instruction in Mixed-Ability Classrooms.* Alexandria, VA: Association for Supervision and Curriculum Development (ASCD), 2001.

Chapter 6

Learning to March in Formation—Cooperative Learning

Cooperative learning or chaos?
Is there really a difference?

One of the most exciting developments in modern education goes by the name of cooperative (or collaborative) learning and has children working in pairs or small groups. An impressive collection of studies has shown that participation in well-functioning cooperative groups leads students to feel more positive about themselves, about each other, and about the subject they're studying. Students also learn more effectively on a variety of measures when they can learn with each other instead of against each other or apart from each other. Cooperative learning works with kindergartners and graduate students, with students who struggle to understand and students who pick things up instantly; it works for math and science, language skills and social studies, fine arts and foreign languages.

— Alfie Kohn

From My Experience

Many years ago I was invited to address a teacher group about the benefits of using cooperative learning in the classroom. I explained the general concept of utilizing small groups of students engaged in specific learning tasks to achieve a common goal. One veteran teacher leaned back in his chair and announced to us all, "Yeah, we used to have that in my day, only back then it was called cheating." We all laughed, but I could see he was serious.

I showed them a complicated picture showing a tray covered with many unrelated objects. I asked the participants to memorize the objects on the tray and left the projector on for 20 seconds. Then I asked each person to list what she or he had seen. I admonished them not to cheat by talking to each other or by looking at each other's papers.

After about three minutes, most participants were very frustrated with their lack of ability to recall many of the details. I invited them to form groups of four and pool their memories to come up with a group picture. In every case, the list completed by the four members had more detail and was *more accurate than any of the individual lists. When I asked the participants why this was so, they told me that the others had seen things they hadn't seen or hadn't remembered.*

"Exactly," I responded. "That's one of the reasons businesses are moving towards more teamwork to accomplish goals, and schools are using more cooperative learning."

Well-planned cooperative learning activities provide a complement to differentiated instruction. This inclusive teaching strategy emphasizes collaboration rather than competition and thus, allows students to grow in self-esteem and academic achievement. Learning tasks are designed with different levels of complexity to challenge each child to learn something he or she did not know before; thus, teachers can *raise the bar* for all. Individual contributions are enhanced and supported by feedback from the group. Group members' collected intelligences and styles allow students to capitalize on their own strengths while assisting others in areas where they are not so strong. In the process, students learn about cooperation, equity, and the value of diversity.

Traditional Classroom	Cooperative Classroom
Learners are passive	Learners are active
Students work alone	Students work with 1 to 4 partners
Teacher directs work	Students direct work
Silence is valued	Learning noise is appropriate
Teacher initiates discussion	Students initiate discussion
Some students do not participate	All students participate
Individual accountability	Individual and group accountability
Independent learners	Interdependent learners
Affirmations come from teacher	Affirmations come from peers
Individual materials needed	Shared materials

What is Cooperative Learning?

Cooperative learning is an instructional strategy that utilizes small groups of students working together and helping one another on specific learning tasks with an emphasis on group members' interdependence. Whether self-selected or teacher-selected, regular cooperative groups function in a basic self-sustaining manner. Please note, all small group instruction is not cooperative learning. In differentiated instruction teachers often use informal, flexible groups to pull together homogeneous learners for additional instruction, practice, or drill. The teacher is the leader of the group and does not necessarily follow the cooperative model.

Cooperative learning is characterized by activities that:

- *Require students to depend on one another for success.*
  Having students sit side by side working on something they could just as easily do by themselves is not cooperative learning. Students must be required to share materials, knowledge, time, talents, and effort (or any combination of these).

- *Provide for individual accountability.*
  Group members share jobs and make group presentations. Group members are tested individually and/or tested as a group to ensure that each person has mastered the required learning.

- *Utilize face-to-face interaction among students.*
  For all group work, students are arranged in close proximity of each other. They can be at tables, in desks or chairs pushed together, on the floor, or virtually anywhere they can do the task at hand separated from other groups.

- *Focus on interpersonal and group skills.*
  Tasks are designed to include such components of positive interpersonal communication skills as active listening, building consensus, sharing, supporting, restating, using appropriate eye contact and gestures, and encouraging. Teams learn to stay on task and check with team members for understanding.

Why Use Cooperative Learning?

The business world has repeatedly told educators that the two most important skills they want in employees for the 21st century are (1) the ability to solve problems creatively and (2) the ability to work together to achieve a common goal. School mission statements usually include references to students being caring members of the community, and being non-judgmental towards others. Having students participate in various heterogeneous group arrangements is an exceptional way of getting them to talk to one another in a positive environment. Students with learning disabilities, poor language skills, physical impairment, and other challenges are able to get support from their peers, as well as contribute to all group members' capacity for tolerance.

Purposeful cooperative learning activities help students develop interpersonal communication skills they will need later for marriage, jobs, families, friendships, and other social interactions. Intentional socialization components woven into learning activities help build a sense of community and common purpose for students. Chapter 7 will give more information about this emotional literacy consideration.

Thirty years of research has shown that when cooperative learning is used effectively, students achieve higher levels of thinking, retain more of what they learned, assume greater responsibility for their own learning, and have more affirmative feelings about school, as well as the particular subject matter. Low-level, middle-level, and high-level learners all demonstrate positive gains in cognitive transfer when cooperative learning is used as an instructional strategy.

If you want to be incrementally better:
   Be competitive.

If you want to be exponentially better:
   Be cooperative.

— Unknown

Benefits of Cooperative Learning

- Increase achievement at all ability levels
- Empower students to take responsibility for their own learning
- Improve retention
- Generate more positive feelings towards the subject matter
- Provide more active learning
- Focus more time on learning
- Lower frustration and anxiety among students
- Enhance a sense of community among students
- Promote interpersonal communication skills
- Boost feelings of self-worth

How to Use Cooperative Learning

At one time I believed that cooperative learning was an appropriate strategy for any student beyond the fourth grade. I hadn't considered using this strategy for younger children because my favorite model is a bit sophisticated for them. Often times when I worked with younger students they had so much difficulty with the process that they missed the content.

Then I began coaching lower elementary teachers who were using cooperative learning quite effectively. The secret was that they used a different model! Most of them introduced cooperative learning as a strategy between only two students. After the children mastered the techniques of working and sharing in pairs, the teachers sometimes grouped them in groups of three or more. Many times teachers assign an activity for *pairs and then have each pair combine with another set of pairs and so on until the group is as large as eight.*

There are several successful models to aid teachers in developing strategies to illustrate positive social values and behaviors. Foyle, Lyman, and Thies (1992) found that younger learners need:

- appropriate experiences (with modeling)
- adequate time
- opportunities to process the experience

With intermediate, middle level, and secondary learners, groups of four or five work well. Depending on the time available, the difficulty of the task, the room arrangement, and the familiarity of the students with cooperative learning, the numbers of group members may vary. Stay away from groups larger than five because, in most cases, groups of six or more tend to break into subgroups, and it is difficult to create specific jobs for more than five. Try these guidelines, but adapt them for your own situation.

In working with older learners, it is important to remember that:

- Group members are responsible for the performance of each individual learner.

- Group members are individually accountable and must be able to report on or explain the team's results.

- The groups are to be assigned by the teacher. Their make-up should be heterogeneous with respect to sex, race, socioeconomic status, ability/learning styles, cliques, and other important factors.

- Leadership is shared on a rotating basis. Each team member has a job and responsibilities.

- The teacher is a resource; students are in charge of their own learning.

- Time must be allowed for group processing and self-evaluation.

Addressing Common Concerns About Cooperative Learning

Educators, administrators, and parents have expressed concerns about cooperative learning in the classroom. Here is a list of ten of the most common concerns, with responses supported by research and my experience.

COOPERATIVE LEARNING CONCERN # 1

"The same students end up doing most or all of the work."

Students engaged in well-run cooperative learning activities each have a specific job. Here is an example of a successful management plan for assigning and supervising the jobs. The jobs rotate every time a new activity is assigned. Each student's seat has one of four colored dots (red, blue, yellow, or green) permanently stuck to it. On the wall are quarter-size posters with the name and responsibilities of each of the individual jobs: Materials Manager, Group Leader, Timekeeper, and Data Collector. Use the fifth job, Encourager, if a team has five members. On each of the job posters there is a small Velcro™ tab at the bottom right edge. Stuck to the Velcro™ tab on the poster is a laminated circle (red, blue, yellow, or green). At the beginning of the activity, students look to see which job has a color dot to match the one on their seats. The matching dot is their job assignment for the lesson. Rotate the jobs by switching the circles on the posters before each activity to ensure that students have a chance to do all the jobs on an equal basis. Students participating in self-selected groups may want to decide on job assignments among themselves.

Provide a set of small laminated job placards for each group. Reproducible patterns for these placards are provided on pages 214 and 215. The placards are placed in front of the students. On the side that faces away from the student is the name of the job; on the side that faces toward the student are the job responsibilities. These placards help remind the students of their jobs for the day, and help the teacher see if team members are performing their assigned tasks.

Data Collector

1. Collects data for acti
2. Records data on appropriate form o
3. Returns data shee teacher and/or re group data on cl sheet
4. Ensures all oth members check data she
5. Helps with clean-up

Data Collector

Base part of the group's participation grade on how well each team member performs his or her job. Deduct points if one team member usurps another team member's assigned responsibility. In this way, each student is required to experience being the leader, being the person who writes the data, being the person who keeps others on task, and being the person who handles the materials. Since all team members must sign off on the completed data sheet (activity sheet, project report, etc.), everyone is involved in the process.

The fact that only the group leader can ask questions of the teacher keeps a highly verbal student from always being the one to interact with the teacher. It is also helpful in restricting superfluous questions of the teacher since the team must discuss among themselves first, before posing the problem to the teacher. Often they find the answer among themselves.

This model has no reporter job, so students never know ahead who will be responsible for answering questions, making the report, or presenting the data. All team members must work together to ensure that everyone knows the material equally well.

I usually choose a color at random to assign the reporter for the activity. This model has been extremely successful for me in making sure that all students in each group participate, and that no one student ends up doing all the work. I also monitor the groups as they work to ensure that students do their jobs.

COOPERATIVE LEARNING CONCERN # 2

"The teacher will lose control in the class."

The best way not to lose power is to give it away. Putting students in charge of their own learning is an extremely effective way of managing a class. Generally teachers who do not ordinarily have classroom management problems with whole groups will not have management problems with small groups. Unfortunately, the opposite is also true.

However, these tips can help with management issues:

- Have all materials ready and sorted before students arrive. Use paper box lids, plastic trays, or plastic tubs to hold necessary supplies.

- Practice routines and procedures for cooperative learning before starting rigorously challenging graded assignments.

- Take it slowly. Prepare students for cooperative learning by doing team-building activities first. Plan extra time for debriefing social issues at the end of activities.

- Closely monitor groups and use the group participation number line to remind students about inappropriate behavior.

Use this strategy for well-controlled cooperative learning. When the Materials Manager picks up the materials, a copy of the Group Participation Number Line is included. The Data Collector fills in the date, group number, and group members present and places the Number Line in an accessible place for the teacher. As the teacher monitors the groups, the teacher will note any infractions of procedural or management standards by marking through the highest number not yet marked (100 is always first). A reproducible participation number line is provided on page 216.

Group Participation Number Line

Date: _____ Group Number: _____

Group Members Present:

_____   _____
_____   _____
_____   _____

100 95 90 85 80 75 70 65 60 55 50 45 40 35 30 25 20 15 10 5 0

Participation Points Earned:_____

I take off points if one student is doing another student's job.
At the end of the activity, the Data Collector (or the Encourager, if there is one) notes the highest number that is not marked through and enters it on the bottom line. This number represents the group's participation points.

The participation points are then averaged in with the activity score. The weight of the participation grade is up to the teacher. Participation may be 100% of the grade when doing introductory activities; later on it can be dropped to 50%, 25%, or lower. Teachers should be the judge of what works in terms of their short-term and long-range goals for students.

COOPERATIVE LEARNING CONCERN # 3

"It is difficult to keep students on track."

Use these two strategies to keep students focused. One strategy is to pay close attention to students as they work. Monitor and mark off points on their number line for off-task behavior. Another effective strategy is to give the students a set number of minutes to complete their tasks and to have the Timekeeper keep up with the time. Use stopwatches for this purpose, or have students use their own watches or a classroom clock. Periodically the teacher should say, "Timekeepers, watch your time."

(Of course, occasionally you will have that concrete sequential student who takes his job too seriously. You will hear him telling his group, "We have 2 minutes and 55 seconds left . . . 54 . . . 53 . . . "
I usually place a gentle hand on his shoulder and whisper, "Chill out, son, you are working way too hard!")

COOPERATIVE LEARNING CONCERN # 4

"Some students will undermine the group's success."

One of the easiest solutions to handling a problem team member is to remove the student from the assigned group and make that person a group of one. Require the student to do the same assignment in the same amount of time as the others. If the learning task has been structured in a true cooperative manner (and it always should be), the solitary student will be unable to produce a quality product alone and will suffer the penalty of reduced credit for the assignment.

I have had students beg me to be put back on a group after this consequence.

A more proactive approach is to talk with individual students who seem to have difficulty relating to and cooperating with their peers. Here is an example to illustrate how this approach works.

I once had a student, Doug, who was extremely intellectually gifted and had zero patience with those who were not as quick. At his worst, he was extremely rude and stubborn.

At his best, he patronized and controlled the others. He openly stated that he did not want to be in anyone's group. When I put him in a group he would purposely try to get participation points taken off to punish his teammates for ignoring him. No one wanted to have him in a group.

In keeping with my focus on short-term and long-range goals, I considered Doug. I knew that he was very insecure about his peer relationships and that he used his superior intellect as a defense mechanism. I did not want him to continue to disrupt his groups and cause them to lose points. Doug had a lot to offer his peers, but he desperately needed some help with his relationships.

One day before I assigned new groups, I asked three female students to join me in the hall. I believe in being up front with my students, and I told them the truth: "Girls, tomorrow I am going to assign new groups, and I am putting Doug in with you three." They all groaned and rolled their eyes.

I said, "I know that Doug can be difficult. I have given this a lot of thought, and I tried to come up with the three most affirming, patient, compassionate students I know. You are the three that came to mind. I know it won't be easy, but Doug really needs someone to reach out to him, and I was thinking that you are the best three that can do it. Anytime you feel like you can't take it anymore, you can come and talk to me. I will support you every inch of the way. Personally, I think Doug is worth the effort. Will you give it a try?"

They all agreed. I placed Doug in their group and closely monitored their interactions. The girls did not let me down. They affirmed him, they were patient with him, and they encouraged him. Often when I walked by, one of them would wink at me to let me know that the team was doing well. Sometimes I would write each of them notes thanking them for their efforts. Soon Doug was working *successfully with his group. I told Doug that I noticed how well he was doing with his new group. When it was time to assign new groups, I got a letter from the four asking if they could remain together for another round—they told me they wanted to keep their "family" together!*

It is important to remember that many students really do prefer to work alone. Opportunities to do solitary projects (at no penalty) should be available for learners at least occasionally. Loners, too, deserve a reasonable chance at success.

COOPERATIVE LEARNING CONCERN # 5

"Giving a group grade is not fair to some group members."

Like some teachers who really don't understand the true meaning of cooperative learning, many parents are confused. They believe cooperative learning will mean that some of the *not so smart* kids will pull down their child's grade or that their child will end up doing all the work.

The first thing I do is assure parents and students that grades will come from a multitude of sources. I do grade cooperative learning activities, but I also grade independent projects, individual tests, individual assignments, portfolios, and alternative assessments. I inform them that, in general, cooperative activity grades are higher than individual scores. If they question a cooperative learning grade, I always have the activity sheets that have been signed by each group member (including their own child).

If the complaint is about heterogeneous grouping, I am quick to tell parents that part of my job is to help students learn to get along with one another. I purposely design many of my class activities to teach and reinforce socialization skills. For parents of children identified as gifted who are afraid that the "lesser" children will slow their own child's progress, I show them the research that has proven all ability levels benefit from heterogeneous grouping. I explain to them about multiple intelligences and point out that students have strengths in different areas. One area that is notably lacking in many students identified as gifted is the interpersonal communication skill intelligence. Some of the highest suicide rates are among gifted students. I let them know that I see it as my responsibility to address the whole student by building a classroom community, and heterogeneous grouping is one way to facilitate that end. Additionally, I point out that, on occasion, students will be given the option of working alone.

COOPERATIVE LEARNING CONCERN # 6

"Group members argue with one another and waste time."

Teachers who do not take the time to practice procedures and routines for cooperative learning are asking for trouble. Unless students have had previous experience with effective cooperative learning practices, they are not likely to understand the expectations. It is well worth the teachers' time to purposefully go through the process with students at the beginning of the year as they are assigned to base groups. Fun activities can be used to acquaint students with rules and rituals.

In order to keep base groups fresh and enthusiastic, it is important to change them periodically. Younger students need a change more often. Older students can change base groups every grading period.

When our district went from six-week to nine-week grading periods, I found that my sixth grade students needed to change groups more than four times during the year. I changed their groups twice during the grading period, and that seemed to work well. You will have to decide what is best in your case.

Remember that every time a teacher changes base groups, the group will have a different chemistry, and the teacher will need to provide experiences for students to bond with their new teammates. Even after sharing several months in the same classroom, students have not been in the same exact groups. They still need to do one or two team-building activities before being assigned more intense academic tasks. Here is a good team-building activity. The reproducible activity sheet is found on page 217.

Common Attributes Game

Once participants are arranged in groups, ask one member to be the recorder and write down each individual's name. A group leader should help the members discover ten (hopefully, unusual) common attributes. At the end of the activity, one person from each group (chosen by the instructor) will introduce each group member and read their group's top five common attributes.

Hopefully, as students later move to flexible grouping situations, they will transfer the skills and techniques for cooperative work that they learned in their base groups.

COOPERATIVE LEARNING CONCERN # 7

"Cooperative learning preparation takes too much time."

Unfortunately, a lot of teachers try cooperative learning only once or twice and are so concerned about the immense amount of time involved that they write it off as undoable. In the beginning stages, as students learn and practice the necessary steps, the going may be a bit slow. However, continued focus and training will eventually result in time saved. Because the teacher will be able to move freely about the room to clarify and re-teach without disturbing others, time will eventually be maximized.

It is true that cooperative learning requires the teacher to spend some time on preparation, but that is done before the students are present so class time is not lost. Students can be enlisted to clean up and set up for the next class so that teachers can actually save time usually spent managing materials.

COOPERATIVE LEARNING CONCERN # 8

"Materials are lost during cooperative learning activities."

When teachers have their prized materials out in the classroom, they sometimes worry that their *stuff* will get misplaced or removed. There is very little chance of that happening when one of the group members is responsible for tracking materials. The Materials Manager (MM) picks up a list of everything that should be in the tub of materials. Then the MM checks to make sure that all materials and supplies are present before taking the items to the group. When the activity is over, it is the responsibility of the MM to check to make sure that all the materials and supplies are back in place and to reset them for the next class. The MM immediately reports any missing or broken items to the teacher.

I once had an overzealous MM who wanted to do a strip search on his team members because of a missing magnet. I denied the request. We later found it stuck to a piece of metal on the underside of the table.

COOPERATIVE LEARNING CONCERN # 9

"Different learning rates make group activities difficult."

Indeed, students do work at different paces, and so do groups. It is never a good idea to have students sitting idle waiting for others to finish. Whether working with large groups, small groups, or individuals, teachers always should have purposeful challenging activities ready for early finishers.

For times when I want groups to work closer to the same speed, I do what I call Directed Cooperative Learning. Students are given the complete set of written steps, but there are stop signs after certain sections.

My instructions to the students are something like, "Go ahead and do Parts A & B and then work on the supplementary activity until I give you the go ahead." I then monitor the groups until most have finished the designated parts before I say, "I am now going to ask the students with green dots on their desks to share what your groups found." When we have thoroughly explored those parts, I say, "Now do Part C and stop. If you have extra time you can begin filling out your activity log." And so on. By directing students to do certain parts and stop, I am better able to informally assess as we go along and adjust my teaching accordingly.

COOPERATIVE LEARNING CONCERN # 10

"Cooperative learning groups create chaos."

There is nothing chaotic about cooperative learning that is well-planned and well-managed. Teachers should plan activities that are challenging, and yet doable, if the group members work together. Tasks should require the concentrated efforts of all team members doing their jobs and working within the allotted time. Materials and supplies should be out and sorted before students arrive. During the cooperative learning activity, it is the responsibility of the teacher to monitor the students and:

- Give immediate feedback and reinforcement for learning.
- Re-teach certain concepts if necessary.
- Clarify directions.
- Encourage oral elaboration.
- Affirm positive interactions and efforts.
- Informally assess student learning and collaboration.

Another way to ensure that the cooperative learning activity is organized and has smooth closure is to allow time after clean-up and whole group information sharing to ask the groups to evaluate how they interacted with one another. Either verbally or in their journals, students can answer questions like these:

- How involved were each of your team members in the decisions your group made? Be specific and give examples.
- How do you feel about the work your group did today? Why?
- What would you like to tell your teammates about how you felt during today's activity, or the way you feel now?
- What could your team do to improve the way you get along and/or work together?
- What is your favorite thing about being on this team?

Teachers need to keep a close watch on the personal interactions going on within groups. Happy, well-functioning groups, matched with appropriate tasks and given adequate time constraints, run smoothly.

Helping Students with Socialization

As teachers gain more experience, they will learn to do more than one thing at a time. A sponge activity, designed to engage students as they walk in the door, will be revisited as a learning activity sometime during the class period. A cooperative learning activity can be used to reinforce social skills while also working on content knowledge.

Whenever I can, I give students a socialization skill to work on in their groups, along with whatever cognitive task I have assigned. For instance, when students are first assigned to their groups, I tell them that I will be tallying the number of times I hear them use each other's correct first names. As I monitor, I carry a clipboard and keep a tally for each group. After all the debriefing on the activity, I announce the winning group and give a small prize.

Other socialization skills that I reinforce this way are:
- *rephrasing what a teammate says before making your own statement*
- *positively affirming and encouraging one another*
- *taking turns*
- *sharing materials*
- *listening attentively to one another*
- *building consensus*

Additional Ways to Use Cooperative Learning

Here is a list showing some great ideas for integrating cooperative learning into everyday plans.

1. **Within a lecture or presentation:**
   The teacher is discussing, modeling, or explaining something. The teacher pauses and asks small groups to summarize, categorize, debate, describe, or otherwise react to the presented material.

2. **With higher level questioning:**
   The teacher asks small groups to come up with a team consensus on something to do with analysis, synthesis, or evaluation of the concept being discussed.

3. **As practice reinforcement:**
   The teacher asks students to get with their groups to practice, memorize, or review the given concepts.

4. **Decision-making/problem solving:**
   The group is to solve a problem presented by the teacher. For example, the school is having a problem with litter in the common areas. She asks small groups to meet and decide on ways the problem might be addressed successfully. Groups report back, a class consensus is determined, and a report is sent to the Student Council or the principal. Cooperative groups can help make decisions about classroom procedures and policies democratically.

5. **As a review:**
   The teacher asks a question. Team members put their heads together to discuss the answer. The teacher calls out a color, and the person who has that color dot will answer the question as the teacher whips through the groups.

6. In a tournament or game format:

There are several models for using cooperative learning in a tournament or game format. Student Teams-Achievement Divisions (STAD) and Teams-Games-Tournament (TGT) are two of the more popular ones.

7. With peer editing:

Team members proofread each other's work and offer suggestions for improvement. This practice helps both the "corrector" and the "corrected."

8. As an assessment:

A Gallery Walk (sometimes called Carousel Walk) is a way to assess students in groups. The teacher puts large pieces of newsprint around the room. On the top of each is a question for which there are several answers. Student groups are given different colored markers and asked to write one correct response to each question. Answers cannot be repeated on a page. The teacher can informally assess student learning by listening to them as they "think out loud" in their groups. (Slavin calls this oral elaboration.) Or teachers can more formally assess the responses by noting the flow of answers used by each colored group.

9. Research projects or group investigations:

Group work on projects can promote sharing of the load and commitment to a timeline. Often students who are procrastinators when it comes to doing their own work will get motivated by their peers to finish their part of the assignment.

10. Checking homework:

Even though homework is for independent practice, many teachers have limited time for checking and correcting it during a rushed day. Group members can check each other's work for accuracy.

Summary

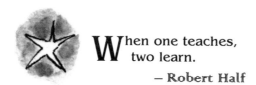

When one teaches,
two learn.

— Robert Half

The use of small group interactions is a powerful teaching tool that can be used to enhance the learning cycle and most other effective teaching strategies. Different marchers hearing different songs still need to learn to work successfully in groups when the need arises. Learning interpersonal communication skills helps students to become better citizens. Working in groups helps students *get better together*.

For more information on the specific techniques mentioned in this chapter, or for lessons designed around particular age groups and subject areas, consult your local bookstore or the Internet. Cooperative learning strategies abound.

Recommended Reading List

Johnson, David W., et al. *The New Circles of Learning: Cooperation in the Classroom and School.* Alexandria, VA: Association for Supervision and Curriculum Development (ASCD), 1994.

Foyle, Harvey C., et al. *Cooperative Learning in the Early Childhood Classroom.* National Education Association Professional Library, 1992.

Slavin, Robert E. *Cooperative Learning: Theory, Research, and Practice.* 2nd edition. Englewood Cliffs, NJ: Allyn & Bacon, 1994.

Part Three

Stepping to Your Own Music

With all our science can one tell
how it is, or whence it is,
that light comes into the soul?

— Henry David Thoreau

Chapter 7

Building A Classroom Community

Emotionally literate educators?
Not an oxymoron!

... DEEP DOWN we all know that assemblies, classroom posters, and happy face stickers cannot change a student's attitude toward school or life outside of school. On the other hand, infusing the classroom and the curriculum with resiliency-building experiences can have a profound impact on our students' self-images . . ."

—Richard Sagor

A LEARNING SPACE needs to be hospitable not to make learning painless, but to make the painful things possible . . . things like exposing ignorance, testing tentative hypotheses, challenging false or partial information, and mutual criticism of thought. [None of these] can happen in an atmosphere where people feel threatened or judged.

—Parker J. Palmer

 If facts are the seeds that later produce knowledge and wisdom, then the emotions and the impressions of the senses are the fertile soil in which the seeds must grow.

— Rachel Carson

The Sense of Wonder . . . Where Have All the Children Gone?

Sometimes I look around at the overly made-up, skin-baring, trouser-bagging, flesh-pierced, hip-hopping, too-cool-for-words young people today, and I am saddened by their lost childhood. Some of our students appear to have missed the fundamental delight in just "being kids." Their behavior often comes across as tasteless and without manners.

If adults wonder why children today seem to be acting poorly, they should try doing a little culture check. Watch the television programs they view on a regular basis. Most of the comedy they watch models laughter that comes at the expense of someone else. Listen to the words to their music; validation of violent acts, low tolerance, and disrespect are the norm. Check out the video games they are playing. Children are invited to kill and maim simulated people to win points. It's a little scary out there. Certainly there are some positive programs, inspiring songs, and relatively harmless video games for children, but they are by far less popular.

Today's headlines scream of man's inhumanity to man. Everywhere there is news of corporate thieves, unethical politicians, and flawed heroes. Our children are constantly barraged with negative examples of adult conduct.

Pair the lack of appropriate role models with the breakdown of the traditional family, and it is easy to see why children today seem so conflicted. Parents are working harder and longer to provide the kids with material things. That means parents are home less, are less attentive when they are there, and only infrequently share an uninterrupted family meal with their offspring. For some families, most all of their traditional rituals are a thing of the past. In short, today's children have lost something important—a connection to families, to a shared history, and to each other.

Those who were born before 1965 can probably remember a now virtually extinct category of clothing called *play clothes*. Children of that time arrived home from school and changed into play clothes. This made sense because these children usually had a large chunk of unencumbered time available to just go outside and seriously play. They interacted with their siblings, neighbors, and friends in games that were not highly organized and required no special equipment. There were no uniforms, no referees, and no Title IX compliance regulations. Kids just played. A lot of socialization took place during this playtime. Children learned to get along, to cooperate, and to handle themselves.

Today's children don't have play clothes because generally they don't go out and play. Some children cannot go out and play because it is no longer safe for children to be outside unsupervised. Some children cannot go out and play because they are so over-scheduled into extracurricular lessons and activities that there is no time left for fun. And still some choose not to go out and play because they would rather interact with a computer or sit passively in the presence of a TV or CD player than actually get up and do something.

It's not my intent to comment on America's pop culture here, but I do want to make one point: Today's children are missing an important socialization process, and schools are suffering because of it.

This chapter is about addressing the lack of socialization and feelings of self-efficacy in today's students. It is written to help teachers build a caring community in their classrooms. The basis for this chapter is the time-honored belief that in order for children to learn they must first feel safe and secure. It capitalizes on new evidence about the relationship between cognitive transfer and emotions. It also focuses on the need for teachers to address directly and indirectly the components of social learning.

The education community fully acknowledges that when students come to school unable to read, it is the educators' responsibility to teach them to read. Likewise, when pupils struggle with math, it is the educators' duty to teach them how to compute numbers and solve problems. But what about the children who come to us who don't know how to act appropriately or how to motivate themselves? Whose job is it to deal with those kinds of particular deficiencies?

My belief is that the answer is everyone's job. Some students have more highly developed people skills and resiliency than others, but all students can benefit from a curriculum rich with opportunities to hone their interpersonal communication and their intra-personal awareness competencies (social learning).

Typical Classroom Exchange Bangyerhead Ondewall Middle School:

The teacher notices a young lady crying and asks, "Charlotte, what is wrong?"

Charlotte replies, "Bryan told me my new braces make me look like a geek."

The teacher says to Charlotte, "Well, you don't look like a geek, so just ignore what he says and take out your book." Charlotte continues to cry.

The teacher is annoyed with Bryan and turns to him, "Why would you say a thing like that to Charlotte? I thought she was your friend."

Bryan shrugs, "I was just kidding with her."

The teacher says, "Bryan, how can you call that kidding? What you said to Charlotte hurt her. Haven't you noticed how self-conscious she has been today because she has those new braces on her teeth?"

Bryan answers defensively, "No, I didn't know anything was wrong with her."

The teacher says, "Well, she has been hiding her mouth and ducking her head all morning. How could you have missed that?"

Bryan looks astonished. "I didn't see her do that!"

The teacher gets aggravated. "Bryan, you couldn't have missed it. You're a very bright young man. Now don't sit there and tell me that you didn't know Charlotte was already upset about her new braces."

Bryan is now getting mad. "Well, I didn't! And I don't know what the big deal is, anyway. Lots of people have braces. She won't have to wear them for life or anything! I can't help it if she's going to try and get me in trouble for just kidding her. Just forget it. I don't like her anyway. I'm always the one who gets in trouble for stuff I didn't even do. I hate this class and everybody in it!"

And so it goes . . .

The really sad part about this encounter is that Bryan is telling the truth. He is totally bewildered about Charlotte's response and the teacher's censure. He really doesn't have a clue as to what all the fuss is about. Even though his achievement test scores are among the top in his class, Bryan is socially obtuse. He isn't what Howard Gardner refers to as *people smart*. He doesn't know how to read body language or pick up on visual clues from others. He is unable to put himself in Charlotte's position and discern what she is feeling. He is unwilling to take any personal responsibility for the situation, and he would rather give up on the friendship than try to work it out. In the end, he lets his own emotions get out of hand, and he overreacts to the situation. Bryan lacks emotional intelligence.

Neither Charlotte nor Bryan is likely to learn any of the information about verb conjugation that the teacher is getting ready to present. Both are upset by the disturbing confrontation that just took place. At best, the teacher can try to quiet the two of them so that the rest of the students can get back on task, but those two students have lost this period of learning time.

Is there anything that can be done to prevent or at least minimize situations like this? What happens to instructional time when teachers constantly have to troubleshoot disputes and off-task behavior?

> *I actually had an education professor once tell me that a good lesson plan will take care of any behavior problems in a classroom. (Yeah, right . . . and a well-planned highway system takes care of all your traffic woes.) While good lesson plans are absolutely essential, anytime people are involved, unexpected things always happen—in life and at school as well. Because classrooms are filled with young humans who have unique sets of experiences, expectations, and emotional intelligences (and in middle school there is always that hormone thing), their precise reactions and interactions cannot be predicted, planned, or controlled. That's what keeps it fun!*

Teachers can act proactively to build a sense of community in the class that will help smooth the way through most daily occurrences. Teachers can also put into place methods for handling unexpected events. The key is that a safe and caring classroom community must be shaped from the beginning. Teachers must work purposefully with students individually and with the group collectively to develop their emotional literacy.

In the past, when teachers took time out to work on activities designed to build harmony in the classroom, they were sometimes told that it is best just to *stick to the subject matter*. They were often admonished not to *waste* valuable class time dealing with affective issues. Nevertheless, they persevered with attempts to build unity and a cooperative spirit in their classes, because it was their experience that spending the time deliberately focused on strengthening the affective side of classes eventually paid off in more time on task and greater learning. They weren't sure why some students seemed to be natural leaders or peacemakers, but they realized that all children did not have the same abilities for working together or even for working independently.

Before Howard Gardner helped educators identify student intelligences, they often said that those who had the interpersonal communication intelligence had the *gift of gab*.

> *(Actually my own teachers called my gift a "curse"!)*

Those who didn't have it were dismissed as excessively shy or social misfits. Educators said that those who had the intra-personal awareness intelligence were self-actualized and self-motivated, and those who didn't have it were immature or had an inferiority complex. Educators relied on Abraham Maslow to help them work through the requisite stages for helping students feel self-fulfilled, but they seldom got past number three on the list.

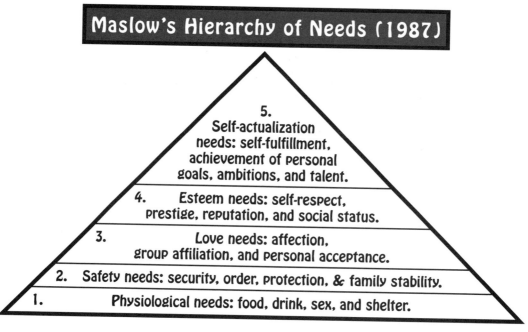

Maslow's Hierarchy of Needs (1987)

5.
Self-actualization
needs: self-fulfillment,
achievement of personal
goals, ambitions, and talent.

4. Esteem needs: self-respect,
prestige, reputation, and social status.

3. Love needs: affection,
group affiliation, and personal acceptance.

2. Safety needs: security, order, protection, & family stability.

1. Physiological needs: food, drink, sex, and shelter.

Then along came a New York Times reporter, Daniel Goleman, who became interested in his and others' observations that the most successful people were often not those with the highest intelligence quotients (I.Q.s). He read research done by Peter Salovey at Yale University and John Mayer at the University of New Hampshire that indicated I.Q. was actually a very poor determiner of eventual success. Mr. Goleman interviewed researchers and psychologists across America, then wrote a groundbreaking book on *Emotional Intelligence* (E.I.). In his research on American students, Goleman found that there is a noticeable decline in social skills that traverses all socio-economic, racial, and gender lines.

What is Emotional Intelligence?

Classroom teachers do not need to be told that there is more violence, less student motivation, and more so-called behavior disorders than ever before in our schools. Most teachers have witnessed a greater number of children who feel sad, bewildered, lonely, confused, and anxious. Student remarks to one another, as well as to the adults in the school, are more tactless and insensitive than ever before. There seems to be an increasing number of children who have trouble recognizing dangerous situations and who persist in actions they know will get them into trouble. Educators are gratified, however, that Mr. Goleman has validated the importance of addressing emotions in all areas of life including schools.

In a 1996 interview with John O'Neil, Goleman elaborated on the E.I. concept:

> *Emotional intelligence is a different way of being smart. It means that individuals know what their feelings are and use their feelings to make good decisions in life. It's being motivated and remaining hopeful and optimistic when setbacks happen. It's empathy; knowing what other people are feeling. And it's social skill—getting along well with other people, managing emotions in relationships, being able to persuade or lead others.*

Goleman goes on to state that at best, one's life accomplishments are only about 20 percent attributable to I.Q. People who possess a high I.Q. are not necessarily ethical, moral, kind, good partners, competent parents, or valuable contributors to society. On the other hand, people with high E.I. are, in general, happier, more successful, and more socially responsible. As a rule, they experience more job satisfaction and harmony in their lives and have less addiction problems. Goleman believes, and many educational researchers concur, that emotional intelligence is at least as important, if not more important, than I.Q. for impacting a person's ultimate success.

While Harvard psychologist Jerome Kagan (1995) believes that the first 24 months of a child's life provide a dramatic impact on how the child will turn out emotionally, his research clearly demonstrates that E.I. can be taught and learned from childhood through adolescence. Many believe that a neurological window of opportunity for emotional centers in the brain extends into the teens. This is heartening news for educators. It is clear that teachers can play an intentional role in helping students master the social and emotional skills they need.

In today's students, there exists sometimes a hidden abuse—the killing of a child's spirit. Children who have not been nurtured or valued understandably often lack resiliency and social skills. The good news is that schools can frequently reverse the effects of emotional deficits. By incorporating deliberate procedures and activities that promote the people-smart and self-smart levels of intelligence in every student, educators can provide emotionally safe classrooms for all.

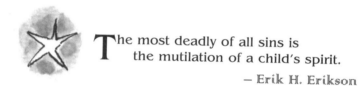

The most deadly of all sins is
the mutilation of a child's spirit.

— Erik H. Erikson

Why is Emotional Intelligence Important?

In the last decade, the emergence of new brain research has given educators more than enough data to support their intuitive belief that cognition and emotion go hand in hand. Learning environments that encourage trust, creativity, spontaneity, wonder, and joy contribute to more motivated students. Research shows that schools that have emotional literacy programs in place (sometimes called character education) have students who are better behaved, pay better attention, and need less discipline. Policy makers should note that achievement scores in these same schools tend to be higher, too.

These findings are not surprising. Common sense demands that students need to remain hopeful and motivated in order for learning to occur. It is obvious that students who are chronically anxious, angry, or otherwise upset cannot keep their minds off the things they are worried about. Their memory centers have limited attention capacity, and emotional needs get first priority.

Eric Jensen (1998) maintains that emotions drive attention, meaning, and memory. He also believes they play an important part in the decision-making process. He reports that E.I. has finally received the attention it deserves because of three recent discoveries in the field of neuroscience:
- the discovery of the physical pathways and priorities of emotions
- findings that the brain's chemicals are involved in emotions
- a link between the pathways and chemicals to learning and memory

Mr. Jensen and others in the educational field now believe there are scientific reasons to explain why it is that when children feel safe their minds expand, tolerance is enhanced, conversations are improved, and more connections are made.

Not since John Dewey urged educators in 1916 to teach "the whole child" has there been such a promising call to action. It has always been the teacher's challenge to create a classroom that focuses on students' social, ethical, and intellectual development. Finally, there is definitive research to support that goal.

The Essential Elements of Emotional Intelligence

- Knowing one's emotions
- Managing emotions
- Motivating oneself
- Recognizing emotions in others
- Handling relationships

Salovey (as quoted in Goleman, 1995)

On Knowing One's Emotions

The child must first learn self-respect and a sense of dignity that grows out of his increasing self-understanding before he can learn to respect the personalities and rights and differences of others.

—Virginia M. Axline

In order for individuals to effectively manage emotions, they must first be aware of them. Many students have been taught to ignore feelings.

When I was growing up my mother often said to me,
"Stop crying, or I'll give you something to cry about!"

Over and over children are told that their feelings are not valid: "You do *not* hate your little brother! Don't you ever say that again," or "Yes, you do, *too*, like to go to church. Now act like it!" No wonder students come to school questioning their own feelings!

Here's a very simple truth about feelings: ***They are!*** That's it, two words—feelings are. No one has the right to tell others how they feel. It is important to let students know that they alone have the power to change their feelings by altering their thoughts. Whether or not they choose to reveal their feelings is up to them, but it is crucial that they learn to acknowledge their true feelings, at least to themselves.

Reading trade books in which characters freely express their own feelings can help start discussions about self-understanding. Students can also be taught to monitor their physical reactions such as rapid heartbeat, welling tears, tightened throat, constricted breathing, sweating, and stomach pains as cues to their true emotions.

Once students learn to acknowledge what they are experiencing, they can decide how to express it and deal with it. Journaling, drawing, dancing, singing, writing, sculpting, talking, and role-playing are just a few of the acceptable ways for students to express their feelings.

(Personally, I like to mount large photos of a certain school
superintendent on watermelons and drop them from high places,
but I don't recommend that to children.)

Being able to label a feeling is the first step to being able to diminish its power. Students should be made aware that feeling an emotion does not mean that they are awful people (e.g., "Right now I hate my best friend, so I must be a terrible human being."). Eventually students can learn to change their thinking patterns in order to master their feelings.

Nagy and Nagy (1999) advise educators to teach students to recognize the "deepest truth about themselves." In other words, educators must constantly give students opportunities to be reminded that they are fundamentally kind, loving, and lovable human beings. When children feel guilty for their negative emotions, it is important that they learn to say to themselves: "I am not a terrible human being who hates my best friend. I am a good person who feels angry right now because my best friend didn't pick me for the team. I need to remind myself about the things I value in my friend so that I can reframe my reaction to this situation."

One activity that works to help students learn to acknowledge emotions and work on the other essential components of E.I. is called *From the Heart*.

> *This is one of my all-time favorite class activities because it can be used in so many different situations.*

From the Heart is a safe, simple way of sharing feelings. It is effective with ALL students, whether shy or demanding of attention. Teachers who use *From the Heart* report that students appear calmer, less anxious, with increased levels of participation and productivity. It is important when fostering a caring culture in the classroom that teachers are open, honest, and frank with students. Likewise, teachers should encourage students to be direct, as well as tactful. Use *From the Heart* to help students through such difficult situations, as:

- a disappointment
- an embarrassing moment
- a fight
- a team loss
- a theft
- the death of a class pet
- an accident or death of a student or staff member

From the Heart

Materials:

Stuffed animal or plush heart cushion

Set-up:

Participants should be seated in a circle. The leader should also be in the circle.

Purpose:

The purpose of this activity is to facilitate communication among students, staff, and others who need to work together. Participants communicate their own feelings and listen to the feelings of others. Cooperation is reinforced through the sharing of individual feelings and the practice of listening skills.

Procedure:

The leader sits with students in a circle (either on the floor or in chairs). One at a time, participants share their feelings or ideas on a topic while holding the stuffed toy. When the student is finished, he or she passes the stuffed animal on to the next person. This continues until everyone has had the opportunity to share. The leader also shares but is careful not to dominate the activity.

Subjects:

Generally it is best to start students with "safe" subjects such as: . . .

- I like it when . . .   – My favorite quality in a person is . . .
- My favorite thing to do is . . .   – I am happy when . . .

Subjects of more depth can be explored once participants build trust among one another and become more comfortable with the activity.

Ground Rules:

1. Only the participant with the stuffed toy may talk. Everyone else actively listens and supports the person who is speaking.

2. A participant ALWAYS has the right to pass and give the animal to the next person.

3. Anything shared in this activity is PRIVATE! Participants should be aware that nothing communicated during *From The Heart* should be told outside the group. Everything must be held in confidence.

4. No one participant should monopolize the activity. Students should be sure that everyone gets a turn.

5. Participants should talk only about what they feel, not about how others in the group feel.

6. The stuffed toy should be handled and passed gently.

7. The leader should also share.

W̲e must structure opportunities into each child's daily routine that will enable him or her to experience feelings of competence, belonging, usefulness, potency, and optimism.

— Sagor, 1996.

On Managing Emotions

Just like Bryan (in the scenario with Charlotte), when he let his emotions spin out of control, students sometimes let their feelings control their behavior. When students acknowledge feelings for what they are, they can control them, rather than be controlled by them. Extreme emotions are seldom conducive to learning goals. Hurtful or violent actions are never acceptable. Students can be taught to handle their feelings appropriately through modeling, role-play, writing assignments, reading assignments, and discussions.

Brainstorm with students about examples of individuals who let their emotions overcome good judgment (road rage, students involved in school violence). Make sure that examples are suitable to the students' grade level and experience. Ask them to generate a list of alternative choices that would be more fitting. Stress to students that while feelings **are**, what they **do** about their feelings is a matter of choice—always. Remind them that while they may not like any of the choices they have, they can at least pick the least unpleasant one and start to work on it. Learning to manage their emotions is empowering to students and acts to help build their overall self-esteem.

Low E.I. students often are unable to delay actions or gratification. A coping mechanism for those who are trying to control their feelings (and/or impulsivity) is to learn to anchor themselves to something pleasing or calming. Much like repeating a positive mantra during meditation, students can learn to visualize a pleasing scene, play a soothing melody in their minds, or use whatever coping mechanism works for them. Provide students with a time-out to regain composure. Counting to ten may not be all that helpful; psychologists now say that a more reasonable time period for calming down is between 15 to 20 minutes.

When dealing with officious bureaucrats, it usually takes me between 15 to 20 hours to calm down!

Educators must consistently remind students that while they cannot control all situations, they can always control their reactions to them. Help students practice staying calm no matter what is going on around them. Teachers sometimes need the practice, too!

The secret of education lies in respecting the pupil.

— Ralph Waldo Emerson

Students with low E.I. tend to feel a need to assign blame to others. They need help in reframing events. **Reframing** is a term that means to try and look at something from another perspective. Just as reframing a picture with different types and colors of frames will make the image seem to change, thinking about a situation from other viewpoints can alter perspective and feelings. In the situation where the child is upset that her best friend did not pick her to be on her team, she could first remember what she values in her friend and then try to see the action from a different viewpoint:

My best friend really worries about other people's feelings. Perhaps she was trying to pick some of the less popular kids for her team and was counting on me to understand.

-or-

My friend has a very strong sense of fairness. Maybe she was trying to let people know that she would not let our friendship interfere with her impartiality in choosing a team.

Reframing allows students to see situations without assigning negative motives or making destructive value judgments. It is a valuable tool for controlling feelings. Teachers can assist students with developing this skill by giving them *what if* scenarios to write about and/or discuss in small groups. Teachers can offer story starters that encourage students to look at an event from different perspectives. Reframing takes practice, but it is a lifelong skill that will serve them well.

No one can make you feel inferior
without your consent.

— Eleanor Roosevelt

On Motivating Oneself

We cannot always build the future for our youth,
but we can build our youth for the future.

— Franklin D. Roosevelt (1940)

One of the most important characteristics to nurture in students is self-efficacy, the belief that they can influence their own thoughts and behavior. It is vital that educators help students understand that the only way they can change their feelings is to change their thought patterns. Discussion and practice are effective means for influencing their ability to take responsibility for their own feelings.

Building Resiliency

Recent studies have examined why children of similar environments and experiences manifest diverse abilities to thrive. Researchers believe that the difference in children's success depends in part on another component of intra-personal awareness—**resiliency**. The quality of personal resiliency has been attributed in large part to a person's ability to motivate herself or himself. While some are able to face great obstacles and failures and not lose their optimism, others are derailed by the slightest adversity. Teachers can be instrumental in reinforcing students' capable responses to difficulties.

Building resilience (competency, belonging, usefulness, potency, and optimism) requires these key teacher efforts:
- Provide students with authentic evidence of academic success.
- Show students that they are valued members of a community.
- Reinforce feeling that students make a real contribution to their community.
- Make students feel empowered.

— Sagor, 1996

Attribution Theory

Teachers have to take some of the responsibility for contributing to the misconception of many students that they are unable to control their futures. When teachers tell students how talented and gifted they are, they are actually undermining student success. What this inadvertently communicates to students is that their ultimate success is based on something beyond their control such as an innate talent. That is not the message educators need to be sending.

Major research on **attribution theory** was done by Wilson and Linville (1982). Attribution theory refers to those causal agents which people feel contribute to or interfere with their success on certain tasks. The researchers found that, in general, people attribute their accomplishment, or lack of it, to one of four things: the difficulty of the task, luck, innate ability/talent, or effort. The researchers point out that the first three factors are externally controlled. If students believe that their lack of success was based on the difficulty of the task, chance, or an inherited aptitude, they are in essence denying any power over the situation. Similarly, if they attribute others' successes to these same factors, they are likely to stop trying because they perceive that nothing they can do will influence the final results. Only one factor, effort, is internally-controlled. Students who believe they can influence their achievements by their own efforts are far more likely to feel empowered and optimistic.

To this end, teachers need to be cautious about their word choices. Let's say a teacher says to a student in class, "Jeremy, you are such a gifted artist. You have so much talent! Wow! I would never be able to draw like that. You are really lucky to have that ability." What has just been communicated to Jeremy, and everyone else within hearing distance, is that the only way to be able to produce quality drawings is to be naturally gifted. If students feel that they are not blessed with such an ability, why should they try?

These words would be much better: "Jeremy, you must be so proud of your work. How long did it take you to do that? Wow! You really spent a lot of time and effort on that, didn't you? That just shows what can happen when you really put your heart and soul into something." With these statements, the teacher has empowered everyone in the room by what was said and by what was implied— most things are possible with hard work. That is definitely a message educators want to send to students.

Something to Hope For

Schools that subtly (or sometimes not so subtly) tell children they will never amount to anything are robbing them of one of the most critical fundamentals all students need. Students need hope; everyone does. It is incredibly paradoxical to see some educators, who clearly communicate to their students that they are doomed to failure, become bewildered when their students won't try anymore. Would anyone?

When I was a child, my mother gave me a small card with the following saying:

> # Essentials For Happiness
> Something to love
> Something to do
> Something to hope for

As long as I can remember, I have had those words posted somewhere close so that I can read them often. These three maxims have powerful implications for educators as they plan curriculums and environments designed to promote life values for students. In building classroom communities, educators must foster a loving environment, pay close attention to what students are asked to do, and be sure that students always have something to hope for.

⊙ ⊞ ⊕ ⊪ ⬙ ◗ ⊙

On Recognizing Emotions in Others

A teacher can help students learn to treat each other well. A good place to start is with building awareness. To learn empathy, a person must first be conscious of how the other person is feeling. In socially inept children, one of the basic characteristics they lack is the ability to use nonverbal language effectively. Some students (like Bryan in the earlier scenario) are unable to read and express emotion in facial expressions, gestures, personal space, postures, tone and loudness of voice, dress, and personal grooming. These inappropriate social behaviors are attributable to **dyssemia**, a difficulty in reading or expressing signs. Often underneath the out-of-sync exterior are intelligent, well-meaning children who are puzzled by their peers' rejection.

Students can learn to read emotions from another person's face, which is a lesson in empathy. Practice sessions, whereby students are encouraged to both model emotions, as well as interpret others' emotions, are helpful in getting them to be more conscious of others' feelings. They can practice pantomiming, as well as reading the seven universal facial expressions: anger, fear, sadness, disgust, surprise, happiness, and embarrassment. Teachers can ask students to watch videos with the sound turned off as they work in groups to infer what the characters are likely feeling. As students become more empathetic, they develop appropriate thinking patterns and hopefully learn to model care and concern for all living things.

⊙ ⊞ ⊕ ⊪ ⬙ ◗ ⊙

On Handling Relationships

Children need to love, to be loved, and to feel valued. When children feel secure, at ease, and happy, they are less likely to act out, be destructive, or harm others. A caring classroom community can help them feel safer, calmer, and more joyful. Without question, teachers must model respectful behavior and a considerate attitude towards students. In order to feel secure, students must feel loved and valued.

An interesting caveat to that maxim is that, in order to be emotionally healthy, children must also be able to give love. Building a caring classroom community requires that students are involved in the process of both giving and receiving caring and respect.

Teachers often worriedly comment on how quickly social skills seem to be deteriorating among today's school children. (For clarification on a part of the problem, I invite them to watch the behavior of their students' parents at ball games, assemblies, and the like.) Students' cavalier treatment of one another appears to be escalating. Distrust, lack of respect, and even contempt are often exhibited in student interactions. Caring classrooms cannot exist where such antisocial behavior pervades.

Corporate America has sent a clear message to schools that they want students to be taught to think independently and also be able to work cooperatively on teams. Not only do teachers have to teach students how to think creatively, they have to teach children how to interact with one another. Students need to learn to be **people smart.** They can learn the requisite skills, but it takes time and deliberate planning on the part of schools in general, and teachers in particular.

On Building Community in the Classroom

Many teachers plan their classroom management programs around a focus on a more involved community of classmates. They use team-building activities that build trust, interdependence, and involvement.

One of the first things I do with new classes is insist that they learn each other's names and something about each other. Here are three activities that you can use to help students learn about each other.

The Name Game

In the Name Game, have each student complete a mini-autobiography card. Use the reproducible on page 218 or develop your own. Students put their names on the back of the card. Later, post the cards and tell students their first assignment is to match the names of their classmates to the information cards. Hand them a separate list of their classmates' names to help with correct spelling.

This activity can also be handed out for homework so that students will talk to each other on the bus, in the hall, and outside of (as well as inside) the classroom.

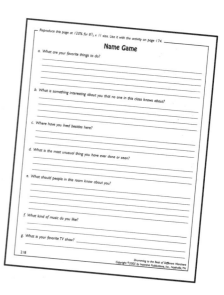

Ball/Balloon Toss

Stand students in a circle. Have a person toss a whiffle ball across the circle. The receiver has to name the person who threw them the object. This game's more fun on a hot day with a water balloon!

To Tell the Truth

Have students introduce themselves by saying their names and three statements about themselves. Two of the statements must be true, and one is a total lie. Other students must guess which statement is the lie. This is a great way to introduce a lesson on observations and inferences, facts and fiction, or other curriculum objectives.

After students have learned classmates' names, you will have to encourage and reinforce their use. Try some of these techniques:

- Take a photograph of each class member. Make a poster with everyone's picture and name. Use the pictures for various activities and reviews.

- Require that students use each other's names when addressing one another. As the teacher, model it (e.g., I think that was a good point, Mark. What did Sheila say? May I do it after Shameka? Randy and Thomas have already had a turn; may I go next?).

- Give bonus points on tests, homework, etc., by pointing to a certain student and having the others write down his or her name.

- Let each student make a triangle card stand (a tri-folded piece of card stock) on which the student can write his or her own name. Students may decorate them any way they like, but they must display them during all discussions, activities, etc. At another time, you may want to mix up the cards and get a volunteer to put them in their correct places. Time the activity to make a contest out of it.

- Don't accept the pronouns "he" or "she" from anyone until they first correctly identify the person to whom they are referring.

As the classroom community develops, continue to use activities that require trust and respect.

The Car Wash is a favorite of mine. In my classroom community, the students will often be the ones who come to me and whisper that a certain classmate is in need of a car wash. They sometimes initiate their own car washes when I am not even around.

The Car Wash

Line up students in two parallel lines quite close together and facing each other. One student is sent *through the wash* (between the lines), and everyone says words of praise, affection, and encouragement. The verbal support produces a sparkling, shiny, happy "car" at the end of the wash!

Run one or two students at a time through the car wash rather than everybody in one big clean-up. This practice ensures that the responses of the washers are fresh, personal, and enthusiastic.

One day, I was having a really "terrible, horrible, no good, very bad day" at school. I was called to the office, and when I returned to my class, my sixth graders had lined themselves up to give me a "car wash." Needless to say, my horrid day quickly became one of my greatest days, as well as one of my fondest memories.

A common problem with low E.I. kids is that they refuse to acknowledge or sincerely apologize for words and actions that have hurt other people. Just as Bryan tried to dismiss his hurtful remark to Charlotte as, "I was just kidding with her," many students fail to understand the cost of their aggression. A really enlightening activity that helps students address this issue is *IALAC*.

This exercise has been around for years, but I first learned of it in Canfield and Wells' book, <u>100 Ways to Enhance Self-Concepts in the Classroom</u>.

IALAC

Each student is given a piece of paper on which is written in big letters, IALAC, along with a plastic bag with his or her name on it. Tell them the letters stand for the phrase, **I Am Lovable and Capable**. Explain to students that everyone in class arrives each day with certain feelings regarding their lovableness and capableness. No one in the classroom has a right to do anything that diminishes another's capacity for these feelings. Explain that taking away someone's capacity for feeling lovable and capable can happen with words, a look, or a gesture.

For the duration of the activity (usually a day), students are to carry around or wear their signs. Each time they feel that someone has done something diminishing, they are to tear off a piece of their sign (little chunks for small infractions and larger chunks for really hurtful things) and give the chunk to the offender. The offender can do nothing but accept and keep the chunk in his or her plastic bag.

At the end of the activity, students discuss how it feels to be disrespected, as well as how it feels to have to accept the paper chunks from others.

Tips for Using IALAC

- It is helpful to role-play the activity as a demonstration with the whole class before beginning the activity.

- Do not send students out of the class with their signs without consulting other adults in the school.

  I once had a furious teacher walk in my room with a handful of pieces of paper demanding to know why my students were giving her parts of their signs. I tried not to giggle as I explained the activity. Boy, was she mad!

- A great follow-up to this activity is teaching students how to make a sincere apology. It is empowering to students to learn to accept responsibility for their actions and to understand how to make amends for their misdeeds.

For great program models of social learning already in place, look at the advisory programs promoted by the National Middle School Association, The Child Development Project (Lewis, Schaps, and Watson, 1996), or any number of the character education curricula being put in place for students K–12. Each of these programs uses prescribed activities that foster positive interpersonal communication skills in students.

Curriculum Connections and Social Learning

As educators build caring classrooms, they must remember that social learning is ineffective when taught as a stand-alone, twice-a-week, or special exploratory unit. It has to be integrated across the curriculum and the school culture. It should be as valued as the cognitive standards and supported by the way in which classes are structured and how the subject matter is taught.

Robert Sylwester (1995) suggests that teachers integrate social learning into the curriculum by using metacognitive activities, activities that promote social interaction, and activities that provide emotional context. He reminds teachers to avoid emotional stress and to recognize the relationship between emotions and health.

A learning space needs to be hospitable not to make learning painless, but to make the painful things possible . . . things like exposing ignorance, testing tentative hypotheses, challenging false or partial information, and mutual criticism of thought. (None of these) can happen in an atmosphere where people feel threatened or judged.

— Parker J. Palmer

Coherent connections between social learning and subject matter learning can be made in natural, meaningful ways. Within their daily and unit lesson plans, teachers of all disciplines can intentionally reinforce:

- self-awareness
- personal decision-making
- managing feelings
- handling stress
- empathy
- communications
- self-disclosure
- insight
- self-acceptance
- personal responsibility
- assertiveness
- group dynamics
- conflict resolution

Eric Jensen (1998) agrees that emotional literacy can be enhanced across the curriculum if all teachers have their students work together to make public group presentations, participate in local apprenticeships, and perform community service-learning projects. He also supports having schools and classes hold more celebrations, use more purposeful physical rituals, and concentrate on novel or controversial situations to engage student interest. He believes that social learning must be embedded in assignments, class structure, discipline choices, and purposeful outcomes.

Emotional intelligence extends beyond the students in a school. Teachers and staff members need to have time to purposefully build their own sense of community and their individual senses of self. Some say that the average child laughs hundreds of times a day, while the average adult laughs only a dozen times. That's a shame because research on laughter has proven that it relaxes the body, lowers blood pressure, boosts the immune system, shuts off stress hormones, and gives perspective. Everyone needs a good dose of humor and playfulness at least once a day. Educators should work on their own lightheartedness and help others find their own sense of inner joy.

- Thoughts Lead to Acts
- Acts Lead to Habits
- Habits Lead to Character
- Character Changes Destiny

 *A Note About Humor*

Emotionally healthy classrooms go beyond establishing a safe and secure environment for all. They are places where there is a shared sense of wonder, joy, humor, and playfulness. Some fear that laughter signals a loss of control, an environment of chaos. Not so. Laughter is a softening influence that helps maintain attention levels, builds rapport, promotes creativity, increases motivation, and boosts retention. Compassionate humor can add to feelings of belonging, as well as create a joy in learning. Students are in dire need of having the joy of learning returned to them.

After several of us were lamenting the dreaded bus duty (on the few weeks of absolutely miserable cold weather we have in the South), I wrote the following poem and sent it to my teacher buddies. We were still cold and aggravated that we had to do bus duty, but at least we could laugh about it.

Duty Calls

You don your flannel underwear,
Roll on three pairs of socks.
You finally find your mukluks,
And take them from their box.

You wear two pairs of woolen slacks,
A sweater and a shirt.
You add a pair of knitted gloves,
And earmuffs wouldn't hurt!

You slip into your down-filled coat,
Pull on your fur-lined cap.
You pocket Liquid Sterno™ cans,
And last, your muffler wrap.

Now dressed, you join the family,
And meet their snickering stares.
They call you "Nanook of the North"
And fall out from their chairs.

You toss your nose into the air
And guess they'll never learn
What are the bare necessities . . .
When BUS DUTY'S your turn!

Recommended Reading List

Goleman, David. *Emotional Intelligence: Why It Can Matter More Than I.Q.* NY: Bantam Books, 1997.

Kessler, Rachael. *The Soul of Education: Helping Students Find Connection, Compassion, and Character at School.* Alexandria, VA: Association for Supervision and Curriculum Development (ASCD), 2000.

Loomans, Diana, et al. *The Laughing Classroom: Everyone's Guide to Teaching with Humor and Play.* Tiburon, CA: H. J. Kramer, Inc., 2002.

Sylwester, Robert. *A Celebration of Neurons: An Educator's Guide to the Human Brain.* Alexandria, VA: Association for Supervision and Curriculum Development (ASCD), 1995.

Thompson, Randy, and Dorothy VanderJagt. *Fire UP! For Learning: Active Learning Projects and Activities to Motivate and Challenge Students.* Nashville: Incentive Publications, Inc., 2002.

Thompson, Randy, and Dorothy VanderJagt. *Wow! What a Team.* Nashville: Incentive Publications, Inc., 2001.

Chapter 8

Paying It Forward

But I'm not even through
paying back my student loans!

A Teacher's Job
by Debbie Silver

All bleary-eyed you check the clock.
Can this be morning sun?
Assignments stacked there still unmarked
And lesson plans not done.

        Last night you sat in graduate class
        And thought of projects due
        And parents needing to be called
        And no time just for you.

You're sponsoring the candy sale,
Composing grants to send,
Rewriting standards for your school,
When will it ever end?

        The mandatory paperwork,
        So much that is required!
        This just can't be the life you chose—
        The job that you desired.

This morning you must hurry up
You've class work to prepare,
A student teacher to instruct,
Observers will be there!

        "I'm so burned out," you cry out loud
         As on to school you race.
        "Too little time—too much demand,
        "What really is my place?"

A student waiting at your door
Tears falling down his chin,
"I need to talk," he says to you,
"Please let me just come in."

        You place your hand upon his face
        With heart about to burst.
        All other things forgotten now,
        Your job is CHILDREN FIRST!

It's Not Just About the Test Scores

Teaching is an incredibly demanding profession. Teachers have to attend to a room full of different marchers while trying to do their own dance to the beat of many different drummers. Someone once likened teaching a roomful of students to "trying to change a flat tire on a moving vehicle." It can get a little harrowing at times. Added to this already overwhelming job is the burden of dealing with a national frenzy for the high-stakes-test-sweepstakes (Popham, 2001).

In June 2002, Secretary of Education Rod Paige issued a 66-page report blasting the teaching profession for being too concerned with how to teach and not concerned enough with what to teach. His implication was that schools could improve their test scores by hiring subject matter experts rather than graduates with education degrees. Raising test scores seemed to be his main area of concern.

Somehow policy makers have finally convinced most of the public that children are better served by the administration of national achievement tests, the ranking of the results, and the comparison among schools for top scores. They have sold the public the idea that educators need to assess only what is easily measured (isolated skills and facts on standardized objective tests), rather than examining how students can apply higher level thinking processes to real life problems.

High-stakes test results are being misused to perpetuate the myth that higher test scores are synonymous with better teaching. But what about the long-range character building and life skills teachers provide for students? Where does that get included? What about the students who take an alternate route to success? When is that success balanced against their low scores on the fourth grade achievement test? What about the student who takes a little longer to *get ready* for the next level? Does the student's delay in achievement count against the 7th grade teacher or the 8th grade teacher? Who gets credit for the student's ultimate accomplishment? Determining what effective teaching is, is just not as simple as the *quick fix* sages out there would have the public believe.

Furthermore, how does one address the dilemma of the teacher who shrewdly coaches the students on how to make better test scores, but in the process destroys their love for that particular subject or their likelihood of being intellectually curious lifelong learners? For an in-depth assessment (pardon the pun) of what America's obsession with high stakes testing is doing to the educational system, read James Popham's book, *The Truth About Testing: An Educator's Call to Action.*

To improve schools, educators must address both the heart and the art of teaching. When I supervise teachers' classrooms, I look at their students' test scores, along with their students' products as pieces of the overall picture. I watch the teacher interact with the students, and I note how students interact with each other. I ask to look at written notes from the teacher to the students, as well as the students' notes to their teacher (or valentines, pictures, cards, etc.). I interview the students and ask them what it feels like to be in that class. Only by examining both quantitative data and qualitative information am I able to tell whether or not good teaching is happening. I think all classroom evaluations should follow this same procedure. It is not just about the test scores.

Changing the World

In the movie *Pay It Forward*, a middle school social studies teacher asks his students to come up with a plan for improving the world. Twelve-year-old Trevor McKinney takes the assignment to heart. He devises a scheme whereby he will do something totally selfless and helpful for three other people. Instead of expecting the recipients to pay him back, Trevor asks each one to "pay it forward" (i.e., to do something for three other individuals). If everyone continues to pay it forward, the mathematical progression will be staggering, and very soon all will feel the world change.

> *The movie is extremely touching, and it made me realize what it is that makes teachers so special.* <u>WE PAY IT FORWARD!</u> *Each and every day, as educators, we give away pieces of ourselves to our students. We invest our time, our energy, and our talent in these young individuals in the hope that someday the young people will* <u>pay it forward</u> *to the world.*

There is seldom any direct payback or even closure to the countless selfless acts educators make on behalf of children. But educators continue to invest in a future we will never see, in ways that can never be measured.

Unlike standardized tests that give an instant (and often unreliable) snapshot of a student's academic progress, there is no test to measure how successful educators have been in fulfilling their mission statements. It is an act of faith that educators continue to give and give with the expectation that their actions do somehow impact eternity.

Educators do not talk about this aspect of the job enough. It is so much easier to get caught up in the mundane tasks of teaching than to look at the awesome responsibility and ultimate accountability teachers have to the future of the world.

> *We should celebrate more! I would love to go into a teachers' lounge and hear someone say, "I think I touched a life today."*
>
> or
>
> *"I think I truly made a difference!"*
>
> or

"You should have seen her face when her classmates gave her a standing ovation for her performance; I don't think she'll ever be the same again."

or

"Well, I think we can count those parents as our allies from now on."

⊚ ⧈ ⊛ ⫴ ⫯ ▯ ⊚

Celebrate Success

I'm not quite sure why educators are so hesitant to acknowledge and celebrate their work. I once sold cosmetics for a well-known all-woman company (mainly to finance my teaching habit), and when we had our sales meetings we cheered, we sang, we told success stories, and we generally bolstered each other in our attempts to make our sales quotas. The meetings were wonderfully encouraging events.

After my invigorating sales meeting on Monday nights, I would go to school, teach, and attend my Tuesday afternoon faculty meeting. What a contrast! All we did there was play the "Ain't it Awful?" and "You Think You've Got It Bad? Just Look at Me!" games. I simply couldn't get it out of my head that at the place where all the celebration was going on we were essentially talking about make-up, and at the place where we were virtually molding the future of our country, we did nothing but gripe and complain.

That has got to change! Faculty meetings should be places where teachers are encouraged to share their innovations, their triumphs, their in-roads toward students' progress, their positive parent interactions, and the humorous things that occur in this intriguing field. If educators are to continue to pay it forward, they need to support one another, to share their success stories, and to encourage one another in this most essential job. In her book, *If You Don't Feed the Teachers, They Will Eat the Students,* Dr. Neila Connors does an excellent job of outlining some very simple things administrators can do to foster such a climate.

Educators who have taught for a while have stories about lives they have affected, and stories about lives that touched them as well. Those new to the profession will soon have their own narratives to convey.

I remember David, a student I encountered during my first year of teaching.

David's Story

David was that child every teacher has experienced at least once. He was an "at risk" student before they had coined the term. His hostility and belligerence were exceeded only by his surly attitude and refusal to let me get near him.

I could have you weeping by telling you David's history, but I don't have to. You have seen or you will see children just like him. He did not have decent clothes, his teeth were not brushed, and usually he was not even clean. This child had witnessed more heart- lessness in his seven years than most of us will see in a lifetime.

One of my colleagues told me not to get my feelings hurt by David's rejection of my attempts to get close to him. She told me that this child, like a lot of our students, was "emotionally bankrupt." She said that every adult he had ever loved or trusted had somehow hurt him or let him down. She told me that the only way he thought he could protect himself was to keep everyone at arm's length.

I tried everything I knew to get close to David, but he was determined to antagonize me in every way he could manage. The beat he marched to was very, very far away. However, I was as stubborn as he was, so I kept on being his advocate and providing him with "tough love."

It finally worked.

On my birthday, after the other children went to lunch, David presented me with a very worn one-dollar bill. He said that his mother didn't own a car, so he had no way to get to a store. The dollar was his gift to me. Looking at his shabby clothes, I almost gave the dollar back. But when I listened with more than my ears and saw the look of pride in his eyes, I took the bill and said, "David, thank you. This is exactly the right gift. I will treasure it always." He ran ahead of me to the lunchroom and proudly announced to my other students that they had all given me the wrong things—what I really liked was "cash money."

The two of us developed a relationship that lasted for years. As a teenager, he was accused of committing a felony. When he was arrested, he used his one phone call to contact me, his teacher, the person who had constantly said to him, "I'll always believe in you, and I'll always be here for you." Even though I couldn't prevent his being sentenced to hard labor at one of the toughest state penitentiaries in America, I was able to write to him throughout his incarceration, to voice my unconditional support for him, and to express my belief in his ultimate triumph.

When David earned his GED in prison, he mailed it to me with a note that said, "I did it!" Years later, he appeared in my driveway with his wife and two beautiful daughters. He told me he just wanted his family to meet me, the one person who believed in him—his teacher.

Educators all have stories like that one. Usually, the times they truly "drummed to the beat of different marchers" are the ones they most cherish, because during those times, they were at their personal bests. In the movie *Pay It Forward*, Trevor McKinney ponders why people hesitate to make the world a better place:

> "I think some people are too scared to think things can be different . . . I guess it's hard for some people who are so used to things the way they are, even if they're bad, to change, because they kind of give up, and when they do, everybody loses."

It's the same with teaching. Educators have to keep trying to do whatever works long-term. They have to be willing to change the things that do not work and keep searching to find the things that do.

Do not give up. Continue to pay it forward.

Educators have to drum to the beat of their different marchers because in the long run, that is what it is all about.

Beat of a Different Marcher

By Debbie Silver & Monte Selby

All children in reach when we find their rhythm—
 The step, the dance, the song within them
That's a better journey, but so much harder
 Too extraordinary, but so much smarter
To drum to the beat of each different marcher.

Bobby marches to the beat of his different drummers
Jeffrey does his reading, but he can't do numbers
Shawna's up and talkin' 90 miles an hour, again
Can't find his book or pencil, that would be Ben

Hyperactive, dyslexic, class clown, non-reader
Upper class, no class, off-task, bottom feeder
Little Arty's a challenge; Martin's a dream
We've seen them all, they all need to be seen.

All children in reach when we find their rhythm—
 The step, the dance, the song within them
That's a better journey, but so much harder
 Too extraordinary, but so much smarter
To drum to the beat of each different marcher.

Sandy's in the slow group, a proven low achiever
She's the small quiet one, not a class leader
Crayons in her hand, she can draw what she knows best
But no room for pictures on the standardized test.

Ballerina, bricklayer, biochemist, ball player
Diesel driver, drum major, diva-destined, dragon slayer—
Some kids have a chance, with a different choice
To show what they know, they must have a voice.

All children in reach when we find their rhythm—
    The step, the dance, the song within them
That's a better journey, but so much harder
    Too extraordinary, but so much smarter
To drum to the beat of each different marcher.

Introspective, oversized, minimized, criticized
Round holes, square lives, not much room for compromise.
There's a new song not yet written
For each and every child, will we listen?

All children in reach when we find their rhythm—
    The step, the dance, the song within them
That's a better journey, but so much harder
    Too extraordinary, but so much smarter
To drum to the beat of each different marcher.
Let's all dance to the beat of each different marcher!

Drumming to the Beat of Different Marchers

Recommended Reading List

Berg, Julie. *When a Classmate Dies.* Fargo, ND: Prairie House, Inc., 1991.

Connors, Neila A. *If You Don't Feed the Teachers, They Will Eat the Students! A Guide to Success for Administrators and Teachers.* Nashville: Incentive Publications, Inc., 2000.

Corrigan, Grace George. *A Journal for Christa: Christa McAuliffe, Teacher In Space.* Lincoln, NE: University of Nebraska Press, 2000.

Popham, W. James. *The Truth about Testing: An Educator's Call To Action.* Alexandria, VA: Association for Supervision and Curriculum Development (ASCD), 2001.

Johnson, Dale D., and Bonnie Johnson. *High Stakes: Children, Testing, and Failure in American Schools.* Lanham, MD: Rowman & Littlefield Publishers, Inc., 2002.

Whitaker, Todd and Beth Whitaker. *Teaching Matters. Motivating and Inspiring Yourself.* Larchmont, NY: Eye on Education, 2002.

Additional Resources

Instruments You'll Need for Making the Marching Music

Behavior Explanation Plan

Student's Name _____

Class/Period _____ Date _____

I violated our class code by: _____
_____
_____

I chose to do this because: _____
_____
_____

A more appropriate choice would have been: _____
_____
_____

This is how I feel about what happened: _____
_____
_____

This is what I plan to do in the future to prevent a recurrence of my actions: _____
_____
_____

This is how my teacher can help me implement my plan: _____
_____
_____

Date _____ Student's Signature _____

Teacher Comments: _____
_____
_____
_____
_____

Individual Behavior Plan

Student's Name _____

Class/Period _____ Date _____

Long-Range Goals for Student: _____

_____

_____

_____

_____

Short-Term Target Goal: _____

_____

_____

_____

_____

What will the student do to meet the target goal? _____

_____

_____

_____

_____

What will the teacher do to help the student meet the target goal? _____

_____

_____

_____

_____

What will the parent or other responsible adult do to help the student meet the target goal? _____

_____

_____

_____

_____

What will happen if the student fails to meet target goal?

1st Time: _____

_____

_____

2nd Time: _____

_____

_____

What positive recognition will the student receive for making target goal? _____

_____

_____

_____

What positive recognition will the teacher make if the target goal is sustained through _____
(insert time period)? _____

_____

Date _____

Student's Signature _____

Teacher's Signature _____

Parent or Other Signature (optional) _____

_____

_____

Comments and Dates: _____

_____

_____

_____

_____

_____

_____

_____

_____

Taking Inventory

Answer every question honestly and candidly. There are no right or wrong answers. All answers will be held in confidence.

1. What is your full name? _____

   What do you like to be called? _____

   Why? _____
   _____

2. List ten words that describe you.

   • _____   • _____
   • _____   • _____
   • _____   • _____
   • _____   • _____
   • _____   • _____

3. List the people that live in your home(s) and put two describing words after each name.

   _____
   _____
   _____
   _____
   _____
   _____

4. What do you think you will be like five years from now?

   _____
   _____
   _____

5. Of all the things you do in your free time, which ones do you like best?

   _____
   _____
   _____

6. Of all the things required of you in your life, which things do you like least?

   _____
   _____
   _____

7. Who is your best friend? Why?

_____

_____

_____

8. What do you and your friends have in common?

_____

_____

_____

9. At what kinds of things do you excel?

_____

_____

_____

10. At school, what are your favorite things to do?

_____

_____

_____

11. At school, what are your least favorite things to do?

_____

_____

_____

12. What is your favorite book or movie? Why?

_____

_____

_____

13. If you could change this school, what changes would you make?

_____

_____

_____

14. If you were the teacher in this class, what five rules would you have?

a) _____

b) _____

c) _____

d) _____

e) _____

15. What is your major goal (ambition, dream) right now?

_____

_____

_____

16. Who is the person you admire the most? Why?

_____

_____

_____

17. What are you most afraid of?

_____

_____

_____

18. What is it about you that makes your friends like you?

_____

_____

_____

19. What is something I (the teacher) need to know about you?

_____

_____

_____

20. Write your own question and answer it.

_____

_____

_____

_____

_____

_____

_____

What I See In My Child

Put your child's name in the center square. Fill in the spaces around his or her name with words that describe the strengths you see in your child. Place the most important attributes in the spaces closest to the center. You can use words from the Strength Word List or your own words. When you have filled in all the spaces, give this sheet to your child.

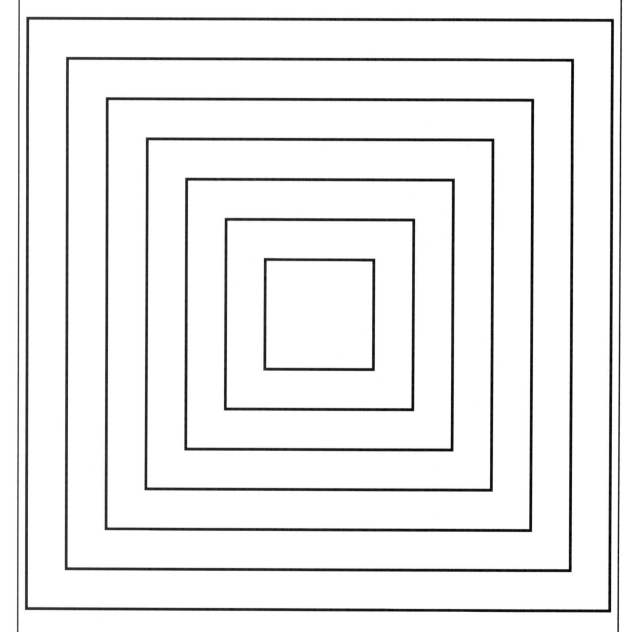

Strengths Word List

Use this word list with What I See In My Child. It will help you get started. Be sure to include words that describe your child's spiritual, mental, physical, and emotional strengths.

SPIRITUAL STRENGTHS	MENTAL STRENGTHS	PHYSICAL STRENGTHS	EMOTIONAL STRENGTHS
romantic	investing	serene	prudent
busy	strong-willed	organizer	confident
kind	motivated	tactful	tireless
artistic	understanding	committed	industrious
careful	disciplined	spontaneous	thoughtful
convincing	self-reliant	commanding	expressive
friendly	persistent	tolerant	settled
gentle	neat	goal-directed	persuasive
loyal	caring	progressive	affectionate
distinctive	thinker	sharp	graceful
perfectionist	clever	capable	reliable
exact	self-determined	certain	leader
tenacious	well-informed	looked up to	growing
balanced	creative	dedicated	eager
ambitious	orderly	courageous	active
outgoing	individualistic	consistent	influential
steadfast	searching	honorable	giving
poised	appreciative	productive	original
strong	fair-minded	determined	thrifty
considerate	respected	planner	unselfish
fulfilled	flexible	efficient	self-aware
manager	likes new ideas	cooperative	self-directed
open-minded	forceful	dependable	adjusted
talented	predictable	comforting	inquiring
witty	intelligent	sociable	practical
systematic	encouraging	serious	unique
trustworthy	imaginative	adaptable	precise
foresight	pursuing	forgiving	listener
empathetic	compassionate	visionary	humorous
cheerful	motivating	artistic	athletic
energetic	disciplined	sharing	caring
daring	risk taker	courageous	patient
coordinated	loyal	fun-loving	perceptive

Helpful Hints for Communicating with Your Child

1. Listen with your FULL attention. For age-appropriate children, a good way to ensure their full attention is put them in the front seat of your car and drive them around as you talk with them. (Unless they want to hurl themselves from a moving vehicle, they've got no place to run.)

2. Be aware of body language, both yours and theirs.

3. Use silence to understand your child's meanings and feelings.

4. Use open responses to keep the child talking. "I see." "Tell me more about that part."

5. Accept and respect your child's feelings. Feelings don't have to be justified, they just ARE.

6. Don't interrupt.

7. Check out your child's feelings by reflecting what she or he says: "I think I heard you say that you were really angry with Susan." "So, you were feeling helpless? Like you wanted to hide?"

8. Be calm. Speak in a quiet voice. Use words economically. Don't talk too much.

9. Stick to the subject.

10. Don't assume that you are making yourself clear. Check for understanding periodically. "Can you tell me in your own words what you think I'm telling you?"

11. Problem solve by discussing a variety of solutions. Emphasize your child's choice in selecting a plan of action.

12. Give your point of view as just that. It's not the law or the only good solution.

13. Don't be a dictator. Remember that children also learn by failing. Once in a while, allow your child to learn successful problem solving by failing.

14. Avoid nagging, threatening, criticizing, lecturing, or probing.

15. NO name-calling! Attack the problem, not the person.

16. Whenever possible, use humor.

How Much Do You Know About Your Child?

1. If your child had a choice, what would he or she prefer to be called? _____

2. Who is your child's closest friend? _____

3. Who does your child most admire? _____

4. Of what is your child most afraid? _____
_____

5. What is your child's favorite thing to do with his or her friends? _____
_____
_____

6. What is your child's favorite kind of music? _____

7. What was the best movie your child ever watched? _____
_____

8. At what age does your child plan to leave home? _____

9. What is your child's favorite color? _____

10. If your child had to wear one outfit for a month, which outfit would it be?_____
_____

11. What most embarrasses your child? _____
_____
_____
_____

12. If your child could change one thing about herself/himself, what would it be? _____
_____
_____
_____

13. If your child could change one thing about your family, what would it be? _____
_____
_____
_____

(continued on next page)

Drumming to the Beat of Different Marchers
Copyright ©2005 by Incentive Publications, Inc., Nashville, TN

14. What trait do you have that your child most values?_____
_____
_____

15. What trait do you have that your child would most like to change?_____
_____
_____

16. If there were suddenly no electricity in the world, what appliance would your child miss the most?
_____

17. What is your child's weight (within two pounds)? _____

18. What was your child's proudest moment?_____
_____
_____
_____

19. What was your child's saddest moment? _____
_____
_____
_____

20. If your child could make one wish come true, what would it be? _____
_____
_____
_____
_____
_____

*Compare your answers with those of your child. Score one point
for each answer that is the same, or reasonably close.*

TOTAL _____

If you score **16 or better**, congratulate yourself for really knowing your child.

If your score is **11–15**, you may want to think about spending more time catching up with what is new with your child.

If your score is **10 or less**, you definitely need to spend more time finding out about what is going on with your child.

About You:

1. If you had a choice, what would you prefer to be called?_____

2. Who is your closest friend? _____

3. Who do you most admire?_____

4. Of what are you most afraid?_____

_____

5. What is your favorite thing to do with your friends? _____

_____

_____

6. What is your favorite kind of music? _____

7. What was the best movie you ever watched? _____

_____

8. At what age do you plan to leave home? _____

9. What is your favorite color? _____

10. If you had to wear one outfit for a month, which outfit would it be? _____

_____

11. What most embarrasses you? _____

_____

_____

_____

12. If you could change one thing about yourself, what would it be? _____

_____

_____

_____

13. If you could change one thing about your family, what would it be? _____

_____

_____

_____

(continued on next page)

14. What trait does your parent have that you most value? _____
_____
_____

15. What trait does your parent have that you would most like to change? _____
_____
_____

16. If there were suddenly no electricity in the world, what appliance would you miss the most?
_____

17. What is your weight (within two pounds)? _____

18. What was your proudest moment? _____
_____
_____
_____

19. What was your saddest moment? _____
_____
_____
_____

20. If you could make one wish come true, what would it be? _____
_____
_____
_____
_____
_____
_____
_____
_____

Now compare your answers to those of your parent. Give your parent one point for every answer that is the same or reasonably close (you be the judge). Your parent has the scoring code.

Outline for Learning Cycle Lesson

Subject: _____

Title: _____ *Grade Level:* _____ *Time Allotment:* _____

I. INSTRUCTIONAL GOALS

General statements of desired outcomes for the learners are phrased to include a process term (verb) and a content term. (Refer to state curriculum standards.)

II. PERFORMANCE OBJECTIVES

Descriptions of specific observable behaviors that students develop as a result of the learning activities. Include objectives for all domains when appropriate: cognitive, affective, psychomotor, and social. For the cognitive domain, include higher-level objectives, as well as those at the knowledge level.

III. TEACHING/LEARNING PROCEDURES

___ A. Motivation/Introduction
Present how you will capture the students' attention, relate the topic to their lives, and/or relate to past lessons.

___ B. Teaching/Learning Activities
Describe the sequence of activities that you will use to teach the lesson.

1. *Exploration Phase*
Identify the open-ended questions or explorations that provide a common experience to initiate students' interaction with information, materials, and/or each other.

2. *Concept Development Phase*
Describe a plan to expand vocabulary, utilize direct instruction, and incorporate the investigation of other resources; connect skills practice to the goal.

3. *Concept Application Phase*
Explain how students will be required to apply new knowledge to "real world" and/or new situations.

___ C. Closure
Clarify the summary of the key concepts in the lesson. Plan how to bring together past, present, and future learning.

IV. MATERIAL/MEDIA

Include a variety of materials other than the textbook. Use materials that appeal to Multiple Intelligences.

V. DIFFERENTIATING INSTRUCTION

Describe any accommodations necessary for diverse learners.
Lesson-related activities can include computer programs, learning centers, activity folders, educational games, peer tutoring, and other methods for helping individual students master the concept/skills.

(Adapted from Louisiana Tech University's Student Teacher Handbook)

Lesson Plan Template

Subject: _____

Title: _____ *Grade Level:* _____ *Time Allotment:* _____

I. INSTRUCTIONAL GOALS

_____
_____
_____

II. PERFORMANCE OBJECTIVES

_____
_____
_____

III. TEACHING/LEARNING PROCEDURES

Time _____ *Activity* _____

___ A. Motivation/Introduction _____
_____

___ B. Teaching/Learning Activities _____
_____

1. Exploration Phase _____
_____

2. Concept Development Phase _____
_____

3. Concept Application Phase _____
_____

___ C. Closure_____
_____

IV. MATERIAL/MEDIA

_____
_____

V. DIFFERENTIATING INSTRUCTION

_____
_____

(Adapted from Louisiana Tech University's Student Teacher Handbook)

Learning Cycle Checklist

In order to make sure a lesson plan follows the learning cycle model, use the following checklist:

Exploration Phase

_____ 1. The lesson begins with an engaging activity, provocative question, or interesting observation that provides or draws on a common experience.

_____ 2. The students are given sufficient time to interact with the materials and/or explore open-ended questions.

_____ 3. Students are asked to collect and organize data.

Conceptual Development Phase

_____ 1. Explanations are based on emerging patterns observed in the exploration phase.

_____ 2. The concepts and vocabulary developed are natural outgrowths of the exploration activity.

_____ 3. Questions have been designed to purposefully move students towards deeper understandings and meanings.

Concept Application Phase

_____ 1. Students interact with one another and compare ideas and explanations.

_____ 2. Students are required to apply newly learned concepts to "real life" situations.

_____ 3. Assessments are designed that allow students to demonstrate their ability to use newly acquired information and skills in novel and unique ways.

Name: _____

Essential Eight

Find someone who can do each of the tasks. Have the person sign on the line. You may sign one spot on your own activity page.

Number Smart

I can finish this numerical sequence:
64, 1, 49, 4, 36, 9, 25, _____
and explain the logic behind it.

_____

Self Smart

I can honestly say that I have more strengths than weaknesses. I can name six strengths in less than 15 seconds.

_____

Music Smart

I can hum the first line of Silent Night on key.

_____

Word Smart

I can recite a poem from memory.

_____

Body Smart

I can put my hands on my head and stand on one foot with my eyes closed for at least seven seconds.

_____

People Smart

I can name five very close friends in less than eight seconds.

_____

Picture Smart

I can recall at least one dream from the last three weeks.

_____

Nature Smart

I can name, within 20 seconds, six ways to sort rocks into categories.

_____

(c) Debbie Silver, 1998

Checklist for Assessing "How" Students Are Smart

Name of Student: _____

Check all the items that apply:

Linguistic Intelligence (Word Smart)

- ☐ 1. Is a good reader
- ☐ 2. Enjoys word games
- ☐ 3. Is a good joke teller/storyteller
- ☐ 4. Has a good vocabulary
- ☐ 5. Enjoys listening to stories and/or poems
- ☐ 6. Likes to write stories and/or poems
- ☐ 7. Communicates with others in a highly verbal way
- ☐ 8. Appreciates rhymes, puns, and/or nonsense words
- ☐ 9. Has a good memory for words, stories, details
- ☐ 10. Other linguistic strengths:

Logical-Mathematical Intelligence (Number Smart)

- ☐ 1. Asks a lot of questions about how things work
- ☐ 2. Has a good sense of cause and effect
- ☐ 3. Finds math games interesting
- ☐ 4. Can see and repeat patterns easily
- ☐ 5. Enjoys working puzzles and brain teasers
- ☐ 6. Understands computer programming
- ☐ 7. Is a logical thinker
- ☐ 8. Can estimate things involving numbers with relative ease
- ☐ 9. Can work math concepts in head
- ☐ 10. Other logical-mathematical strengths:

Visual-Spatial Intelligence (Picture Smart)

- ☐ 1. Reports clear, visual images (or dreams)
- ☐ 2. Can envision objects from more than one perspective
- ☐ 3. Daydreams more than peers
- ☐ 4. Likes to draw and/or create art projects
- ☐ 5. Has a good eye for detail and color
- ☐ 6. Is good at spatial games like chess and Tetris
- ☐ 7. Likes movies, slides, or other visual presentations
- ☐ 8. Can move between 2-dimensional and 3-dimensional representations with ease
- ☐ 9. Can read and/or create maps
- ☐ 10. Other visual-spatial strengths:

Bodily-Kinesthetic Intelligence (Body Smart)

- ☐ 1. Is very coordinated
- ☐ 2. Exceptionally mobile: moves, twitches, fidgets, taps when seated for long
- ☐ 3. Enjoys working with clay, finger-paint, other tactile media
- ☐ 4. Can mimic others' gestures, posture, and movements
- ☐ 5. Must touch anything new or interesting
- ☐ 6. Loves to take things apart and put them back together
- ☐ 7. Uses dramatic body movements for self-expression
- ☐ 8. Enjoys running, hopping, climbing, wrestling, similar activities
- ☐ 9. Exhibits fine motor control (crafts, painting, etc.)
- ☐ 10. Other bodily-kinesthetic strengths:

Musical Intelligence (Music Smart)

- ☐ 1. Can detect music that is off-key, off-beat, or disturbing in some way
- ☐ 2. Remembers melodies of songs
- ☐ 3. Taps rhythmically as he/she works or plays
- ☐ 4. Sensitive to environmental noise (rain on the windows, etc.)
- ☐ 5. Plays a musical instrument and/or sings in a choir.
- ☐ 6. Has a good singing voice
- ☐ 7. Responds favorably when music is played
- ☐ 8. Sings songs that he/she has learned
- ☐ 9. Unconsciously hums much of the time
- ☐ 10. Other musical strengths:

Interpersonal Communications Intelligence (People Smart)

- ☐ 1. Establishes meaningful peer relationships
- ☐ 2. Seems to be a natural leader
- ☐ 3. Empathizes with others
- ☐ 4. Likes to play with others
- ☐ 5. Shows good teamwork skills
- ☐ 6. Others seek this student's company
- ☐ 7. Has two or more close friends
- ☐ 8. Frequently acts as a mediator and/or peace maker
- ☐ 9. Enjoys teaching others
- ☐ 10. Other interpersonal communication strengths:

Intra-personal Awareness Intelligence (Self Smart)

- ☐ 1. Displays a sense of strong will
- ☐ 2. Enjoys playing or working alone
- ☐ 3. Has high self-esteem
- ☐ 4. Has a good sense of self-direction
- ☐ 5. Does not mind being different from others
- ☐ 6. Has a realistic view of his or her strengths, weaknesses
- ☐ 7. Is able to deal effectively with successes and failures
- ☐ 8. Has an interest or talent not readily shared with others
- ☐ 9. Seems to "march to the beat of a different drummer"
- ☐ 10. Other intra-personal awareness strengths:

Naturalistic Intelligence (Nature Smart)

- ☐ 1. Likes to identify & classify living & nonliving things in nature
- ☐ 2. Cares for pets or animals
- ☐ 3. Understands repeating patterns in nature and the universe
- ☐ 4. Seems more "in tune with nature" than peers
- ☐ 5. Would rather be outside than inside
- ☐ 6. Has a demonstrated appreciation for a part of the natural world (e.g., dinosaurs, clouds, rocks, etc.)
- ☐ 7. Likes to garden and/or appreciates plants
- ☐ 8. Understands and appreciates the environment
- ☐ 9. Loves to collect things from nature
- ☐ 10. Other naturalistic strengths:

Adapted by Debbie Silver from *Multiple Intelligences in the Classroom* by Thomas Armstrong (1994)

Cooperative Learning Job Placards

Placards are placed in front of the students. On the side that faces away from the student, list the name of the job; on the side that faces toward the student, list the job responsibilities. These placards help remind the students of their jobs for the day and help the teacher see if team members are doing their assigned tasks.

Materials Manager

1. Collect and return all materials and supplies to appropriate place(s).
2. You are the only one who can retrieve materials and supplies.
3. Make sure everyone has equal access to materials and supplies.
4. Check data sheet.
5. Help with clean-up.

Group Leader

1. Read all directions to your group.
2. Lead discussions.
3. Check data sheet.
4. Help with clean-up.
5. You are the only one who can ask the teacher a question.

Timekeeper

1. Hold team stopwatch or watch the clock.
2. Keep group on task and remind them about time.
3. You are responsible for getting the group to finish on time.
4. Check data sheet.
5. Help with clean-up.

Data Collector

1. Collect data for activity.
2. Record data on appropriate form or sheet.
3. Return data sheet to teacher and/or record group data on class data sheet.
4. Make sure all other team members check data sheet.
5. Help with clean-up.

Encourager

1. Monitor all team members to ensure they do their own jobs.
2. Take responsibility for praising and affirming jobs well done.
3. Record comments and actions that show positive interpersonal communication.
4. Report recorded data to group at debriefing session.
5. Help with clean-up.

Group Participation Number Line

Date: _____ Group Number: _____

Group Members Present:

_____   _____
_____   _____
_____   _____
_____   _____

100 95 90 85 80 75 70 65 60 55 50 45 40 35 30 25 20 15 10 5 0

Participation Points Earned:_____

Group Participation Number Line

Date: _____ Group Number: _____

Group Members Present:

_____   _____
_____   _____
_____   _____
_____   _____

100 95 90 85 80 75 70 65 60 55 50 45 40 35 30 25 20 15 10 5 0

Participation Points Earned:_____

Group Participation Number Line

Date: _____ Group Number: _____

Group Members Present:

_____   _____
_____   _____
_____   _____
_____   _____

100 95 90 85 80 75 70 65 60 55 50 45 40 35 30 25 20 15 10 5 0

Participation Points Earned:_____

Group Participation Number Line

Date: _____ Group Number: _____

Group Members Present:

_____   _____
_____   _____
_____   _____
_____   _____

100 95 90 85 80 75 70 65 60 55 50 45 40 35 30 25 20 15 10 5 0

Participation Points Earned:_____

Common Attributes

List each group member's name:

_____

_____

_____

_____

_____

List your most unusual common attributes. The attributes must be true. They must apply to ALL members of the group. Put checkmarks by your team's five favorites.

_____

_____

_____

_____

_____

_____

_____

_____

_____

_____

_____

_____

_____

Common Attributes

List each group member's name:

_____

_____

_____

_____

_____

List your most unusual common attributes. The attributes must be true. They must apply to ALL members of the group. Put checkmarks by your team's five favorites.

_____

_____

_____

_____

_____

_____

_____

_____

_____

_____

_____

_____

_____

Name Game

a. What are your favorite things to do?

_____

_____

_____

_____

b. What is something interesting about you that no one in this class knows about?

_____

_____

_____

_____

c. Where have you lived besides here?

_____

_____

_____

d. What is the most unusual thing you have ever done or seen?

_____

_____

_____

e. What should people in this room know about you?

_____

_____

_____

_____

f. What kind of music do you like?

_____

_____

g. What is your favorite TV show? _____

_____

_____

Finding Your Own Rhythm for Teaching

A Discussion Guide

A Personal Note from Debbie

My full name is Debbie Kay Thompson Pace Silver. Thompson is my maiden name (My dad and brothers wanted you to be sure and know that.), and Pace is a name left over from my first marriage (actually a starter marriage that lasted 17 years). My three sons are all Pace boys, so they like for me to point out that I, too, was once a Pace. My two stepsons are Silver boys, and they often remind me that I am now a Silver. I have been married to Lawrence Silver since 1990. I realize this is a personal biography, but I did promise these important men in my life that I would mention them.

Probably you will be mainly interested in the fact that I am a real live teacher. I have taught every core subject, almost every grade level, and most every kind of student. I have written this book about teaching from the perspective of a southern female. It contains information I wish I had known when I naïvely agreed to be a temporary substitute in a small, poor, rural Louisiana school over 30 years ago. At that time, I had only 60 college credit hours (none of which were in education), absolutely no educational training, and no intention of ever being a real teacher (a long story). I am thankful that there are no videos of my first few years of teaching.

Despite a questionable beginning, I instantly fell in love with the profession, continued to teach, and eventually earned three degrees in education. I like to think I got better every year I taught. I have 21 years of classroom experience and nine years of staff development and university teaching experience. I have had the privilege of working with schools all over the United States, as well as in Canada and Europe. I have learned many tricks of the trade from truly remarkable students and educators all over the world.

In the teacher workshops I give, as well as in my methods classes at the university, I am constantly asked if the ideas I share are written down anywhere. So this book puts some of the most important information in one place. If you are a pre-service or novice teacher, there are loads of ideas in this book to help get you started right away. I offer what I consider just enough theoretical background to support the recommendations made, because most new teachers are so busy trying to start teaching that they basically want to cut to the chase. If you are an experienced teacher reading this book, you will find fresh ideas, as well as affirmation for the great things you are already doing in your class. In addition, it should remind you that we are all in this together, and bring a smile to your face.

I use a lot of humor in my work, in my presentations, and in my life. Please assume that a lot of the comments that I make (as asides) are written tongue-in-cheek. Stories, poems, and anecdotes are woven throughout the book because that is the way I like to teach. You do not have to read the chapters in order nor read everything in a chapter. Hopefully, you will be able to readily find what you need and start using it. For those of you who are interested in further study, please refer to the recommended reading lists.

I have learned many things on my journey of 30 years as a teacher. A lot of what I have learned has come from listening to my students, from my own research, and from personal reflection. However, much of what I now know I learned from watching and listening to other teachers. I have shared this profession with some of the most dedicated, talented people in the world—educators who are true heroes. There are too many of them to name here, but they know who they are.

You will probably think of more and better ideas as you participate in this most noble profession. I welcome your comments and contributions. I will gladly use and acknowledge your original ideas in an upcoming book. Please contact me at http://www.debbiesilver.com.

Activities and Discussion Questions

Use these suggested activities as part of your faculty book circle, as part of a faculty meeting, or as part of a team activity. Pick and choose to differentiate your discussion as would be appropriate for your group.

Part One—Setting the Pace

Chapter 1
Knowing Your Own Rhythm

1. Draw a picture of a typical student. Label the drawing to indicate such characteristics as personality, learning style, strength areas, areas that need work, and other identifying qualities. Share this picture with your group.

2. Compare your drawing of a typical student with individual students that you teach. How does the drawing match up when applied on an individual basis? Begin a student observation file. Make a note card for each student in your classroom. Record characteristics the students have that are different from your "typical" student drawing. These notes are the beginning of your student observations for differentiated instruction. Keep them and add to them as you progress through this book study.

3. Reflect on a time when you, as a student, felt "out of sync" with the rest of your class. Do you recall any specific thoughts or feelings you had regarding your perceived differences from others? How could a teacher have helped you feel more connected to the group and/or school?

4. Do you ever feel professionally separated from the rest of your teaching colleagues? When? How important is it to be accepted by your administrators and teaching peers? How important is it that you maintain your belief system and your values about the teaching profession when your views differ from those of your peers? Is there room for compromise?

5. Describe the very best classroom you were ever in as a student or an observer. Identify the specific things that made it so appealing to you. Were most of them replicable? If so, what are some of the same kinds of things you do in your classroom? If there are things that cannot be duplicated, tell why and explain what you do instead.

Chapter 2
Developing a System
for Classroom Management

1. Alone or in a group make a Venn Diagram. On the left, list management strategies that work short term only. On the right, list management strategies that might work long term, but do little to solve immediate problems. In the center, list strategies that accomplish both.

   Discuss the value of the items you listed in the center as opposed to those on either side. How many of the items in the center of your diagram do you currently use in your classroom? What factors are preventing you from using the ones you are not using?

2. Examine the list of the ten "Cs" of Classroom Management. Identify the five you consider most important. Give examples of how you exemplify those in your daily teaching. List one "C" you would like to improve this school year. Develop an action plan to help you become stronger in the characteristic you chose.

3. Would students in your classroom say that you are more concerned with "the letter of the law" or the "spirit of the law"? Why would they say that? Would their responses be consistent with how you want your classroom to be? Why or why not?

4. How do you feel about the use of rewards as motivators? Have you changed your position over time? Why or why not? Tell how your current position on rewards in the classroom reflects your long-term goals for students.

5. Take a stand on "No Tolerance" (for any issue) and defend your stand using your long-term goals as guidelines.

6. How are the Behavior Explanation Plan and Individual Behavior Plan (pages 196–198) appropriate for your classroom? What modifications would you need to make in order to use a similar form.

7. What are the essential things you must know about a student in order to teach her/him effectively? How do you find out the information you need to know?

8. When do you do your best reflection on your teaching practices? What would help you maximize your reflection time?

9. If you were more courageous than you are right now, what is the one thing you would do as an advocate for the students in your classroom? What is keeping you from doing that now?

Chapter 3
Adding Harmony
with Parental Involvement

1. Take turns being the parent(s) and the teacher(s). Role play the following scenarios:

   Situation 1: A parent is trying to explain that "boys will be boys." The teacher suspects that the child may have ADHD and need help of some kind.

   Situation 2: A parent is trying to convince the teacher that his/her child has ADHD and needs medication. The teacher does not agree with the diagnosis nor a recommendation for medication.

   Situation 3: A parent thinks the teacher assigns too much homework.

   Situation 4: A parent wants to talk to a science teacher about the teacher's views on creationism.

   Situation 5: A parent wants to make sure that his/her child is going to make the honor roll.

   Situation 6: A parent is sure that his/her child has done nothing wrong, but several other students are "getting the child into trouble."

   Situation 7: A parent wants to discuss the misdeeds of past teachers, as well as other teachers in the school.

   Situation 8: The parent is a former teacher who does not concur with several of the teacher's teaching methods.

   Situation 9: The parent seems totally unconcerned with the well-being of his/her child.

   Situation 10: Create a scenario appropriate to your particular school or situation. Let group participants offer suggestions or ideas.

2. What are some specific things your school could do to make parents feel more welcome in your school? What are some specific things you could do to make parents feel more welcome in your classroom?

3. Compose an open letter (a) to the parents of your students telling them exactly what you need from them to help make their children's school experience more

successful. Do not worry about being "politically correct"; just say whatever you feel. Share your letter with your group. Write a hypothetical response (b) from the parent. Answer your first letter with the excuses, reasons, and rationalizations you would expect from your students' parents. Then write an ideal response (c) you would like to hear from parents. Compare letters for (b) and (c). What could you do to help bring them more in line with each other?

4. On the student observation note cards you prepared earlier (Chapter 1, Activity 2), make a space to record each time you have contact with the student's parents, using a code to indicate the nature of the call. Some time after the first semester create a graph depicting the number and types of your calls. Make a note to yourself to call any parent who has not been contacted with positive news.

5. If you are, or have been the parent of a school-age child, discuss an instance when you felt totally frustrated by a teacher and/or the school. Did that change the way you interact with parents now?
Why or why not?

Part Two—Differentiating Instruction for Different Learners

Chapter 4
Teaching Those Who Hear Distant Drummers

1. Individually or in small groups design a lesson appropriate to your grade and subject area that follows the learning cycle. Use the template provided in the book on page 210, and consult the checklist on page 211 to make sure you have provided adequately for all three phases. Present either your model or the lesson itself to your discussion group. Have other participants comment on what they like, problems they anticipate, and/or suggestions for improvement. Compile a folder of the various learning cycle lessons presented in your group for each member. (Your study group has created a starter collection of learning cycle lessons for your differentiated classrooms.)

2. David Ausubel says, "The single most important factor influencing learning is what the learner already knows." What does that really mean? Do you agree? Why or why not?

3. What is the absolute most successful lesson you ever taught? Did it have elements of the learning cycle? Which ones? What has kept you from teaching like that all the time?

4. Brainstorm discrepant events for a myriad of topics that you teach. Share these with your group members. Make copies for everyone so that all participants have a starter folder of discrepant events.

5. Review the list of Technique Tips for Effective Questioning on page 94. State whether you agree or disagree with each one. Explain what you do that is similar or different and tell why. Support your answers with your long-term goals for students.

Chapter 5
Understanding Multiple Intelligences and Different Learning Styles

1. Copy and distribute the Essential Eight Activity to each group member. Do the activity. Were all eight intelligences represented in your group?

2. Copy and distribute the Checklists for Assessing "How Students Are Smart" (page 213). Tell participants NOT to put their names on their sheets. Ask them to fill out the checklists about themselves honestly and candidly. Post the checklists in a common area and see if your group can guess who filled out each form.

3. Do you know of a story about a student similar to Andy's story (pages 104–106)? Share what happened as you watched that student find an alternate path to success. Is this student's success story applicable to students you have now? Why or why not?

4. Pick a unit topic for any subject you teach. Write eight instructional strategies for teaching the essential ideas of your topic that utilize each of the eight intelligences. Then write an assessment technique that capitalizes on each of the eight intelligences. Share copies of your lists with your group members.

5. On the student note cards you began earlier, write one or two dominant intelligences for each of your students.

6. Do you agree with Gardner's statement, "It's not about how smart they are, it's about how they are smart"? Why or why not?

7. Purchase Gregorc's Adult Learning Style Inventory for your discussion group members from his Website.* Have someone administer the inventory to the other participants. Share results with group members and see if any are surprised by the results.

    *The instrument used for this is workshop is copyrighted and must be purchased for approximately $2.50 per participant. For more information, see http://www.gregorc.com/instrume.html.

8. Chose a topic for a unit of study that you teach. List at least five strategies for each of the four Learning Styles that could be used to differentiate instruction of the unit's essential ideas.

9. Either by looking at the results from your learning style inventory or by reading Gregorc's descriptors, identify your prominent style for processing new information. Describe the things that are easy for you to do as a teacher because of your particular style. Describe the things that are hard for you to do.

10. Which student learning style is the hardest for you to address? Why do you think that is? How can you modify what you are presently doing to accommodate the learners you identified?

11. In your own words, describe Vygotsky's "zone of proximal development" (page 122). Give specific examples of teachers utilizing this approach to instruction. Why is recognizing this area important for differentiating instruction?

Chapter 6
Learning to March in Formation— Cooperative Learning

1. As individuals or as partners, design a cooperative learning activity you can lead for your study group. Have timers, job placards, group participation number lines, and all materials needed to complete the activity. Have group members do the activity using timers, job placards, and the materials provided. Ask them to follow their particular job outlines. Use the group participation number lines to monitor their cooperative behavior skills. De-brief the activity you chose, and then discuss the effectiveness of the cooperative learning strategy itself.

2. In grade level groups, brainstorm a list of helpful tips for using cooperative learning in the classroom. Copy the list(s) and share with all group members.

3. How can a teacher help students transfer the cooperative skills they learn while working together in their base groups to less formal groupings like self-selected, flexible, and paired configurations commonly used in differentiated instruction?

4. What is the ideal composition (size, make-up, etc.) for base groups in the grade level you teach? Think about the job assignments that are appropriate for your students and explain how your choices fit into your short-term and long-term goals for your class.

Part Three—Stepping to Your Own Music

Chapter 7
Building a
Classroom Community

1. Ask each group member to write his/her name on the top of a sheet of paper. Have a group leader collect all the sheets and randomly redistribute them, making sure that no one gets her/his own paper back. Ask members to look at the name on the sheet, then write one or more positive sentences about that person. (All sentences should begin with the word "I" or "You"—no third person pronouns allowed.) Comments should be true, specific, and affirming. As participants finish writing on a particular paper, they may trade with anyone else, as long as they do not get their own papers back. Trading continues until members have had a chance to write on a majority of the papers. The leader then collects all papers and redistributes them to their original owners. Group members read the comments made about them and discuss the value of this exercise for classroom members.

2. Do the Car Wash Activity (page 175) for one or two group members. Afterwards, discuss how it felt to be a part of the activity. List possible times for implementing the Car Wash in the classroom.

3. As a group, make a list of activities and tips for promoting the "people smart" intelligence in the classroom. Copy the list and distribute it to all members.

4. As a group, make a list of activities and tips for promoting the self-smart intelligence in the classroom. Copy the list and distribute it to all members.

5. Have a leader conduct a From the Heart session (page 166) on a current issue facing your school or group. Discuss the helpfulness of this session and brainstorm other possible times to use this activity.

6. Read the section on Attribution Theory (page 170). Discuss the importance of the word choices teachers make. Give examples of unintended consequences of unconsidered teacher comments.

Chapter 8
Paying It Forward

1. Ask discussion members to "Pay It Forward" by sharing with the group particularly meaningful success stories they have experienced in teaching. (For those new to teaching, it can be something they observed or know about.)

2. Discuss how a teacher can find the balance between focusing on students' welfare and addressing the ever-increasing pressure of high stakes tests.

3. Create a poster or banner depicting what the adults in the school can easily do to uplift one another on a regular basis. Display the poster or banner in a place where all adults in the school can see it.

4. Throw yourselves a party in celebration of who you are, what you do, and your completion of your book study! (Be sure to invite Debbie!!)

A Note of Thanks

The idea for this discussion guide came from Park R-3 School District in Estes Park, CO. The teachers there, under the direction of Linda Chapman, formed one of the first study groups to use my book for a faculty book circle. Laura Brown wrote a six-week course of study based on my work. Her great ideas helped in writing this guide. I am eternally grateful to Laura, to Linda, and to the teachers of Park R-3 District for their camaraderie and their commitment to professional development. Thank you, Park District educators, for being advocates for your many "different marchers."

Glossary

Accommodation

Concept used by Piaget to describe the adjustment an individual makes when incorporating new information. Accommodation is the individual's response to the immediate and compelling informational input that has been and is being assimilated (see Assimilation).

Aggressive

Showing a readiness or having a tendency to attack or do harm to others.

Anchoring

Using a conditioned response to elicit a behavior (i.e., eating foods to feel comfort; thinking of a beautiful beach to bring on a sense of calm; listening to a song to feel energetic).

Assertive

Confident in stating your position or aim; forceful.

Assertive Discipline

A classroom management system developed by Cantor. The strategy centers on a discipline plan with a rigid set of rules, penalties, and rewards. The simple set of rules is displayed in every classroom, along with a list of rewards for keeping them, and the consequences of breaking them.

Assimilation

Concept used by Piaget to describe the process of conceptualizing and internalizing one's new experience. Piaget believes that assimilation is a spontaneous process on the part of the child. (Used in conjunction with accommodation.)

Attribution Theory

In the context of student motivation, this theory suggests that students base their explanations of success on external causes (task difficulty, luck, innate ability) or internal causes (effort) or some combination of the four.

Automaticity

Learned behavior that has been so internalized that it can be done without thought or intention, thus freeing the mind to do higher-order tasks.

Classical Conditioning

Term used to describe Pavlov's research on the pairing of a conditioned response with an unconditioned stimulus over time to see if the conditioned stimulus alone could trigger a response. In his classic experiment, he played a tone as he presented meat powder to a dog over and over. Eventually the tone alone (without the meat powder) resulted in the dog's beginning to salivate.

Constructivism

A perspective that holds that knowledge is constructed in the minds of learners based on their prior knowledge and previous experience.

Cooperative Learning

An instructional strategy that uses small groups of students working together and helping one another to complete a collaborative learning task.

Discrepant Event

A perplexing situation that causes cognitive dissonance (inability to understand); like a magic trick that seems impossible.

Disequilibration

Term used by Piaget to describe the cognitive dissonance that occurs when what a child observes is inconsistent with his or her prior knowledge and/or beliefs.

Dyssemia

A difficulty in understanding nonverbal signs and signals.

Equilibration

Term used by Piaget to describe the motivational force for arriving at an adjustment between the twin concepts of assimilation and accommodation.

Extrinsic Rewards

Rewards that come from an outside source such as the teacher. Rewards include the obvious bonuses such as prizes, certificates, special privileges, gold stars, stickers, candy, gum, redeemable tokens, grades, or even money. Teacher praise is also considered to be an extrinsic reward, as are more subtle signs of approval such as "thumbs up" signals, smiles, nods, hugs, and pats on the back.

Flow State

Term coined by Mihalyi Csikszentmihalyi to describe a state of concentrated action and awareness.

Intrinsic Rewards

The inherent or natural consequences of the behavior become the *reward* for the behavior. Some researchers prefer the term reinforcers to rewards because teachers use them to strengthen behavior (making it more likely to be repeated).

Learning Cycle

A teaching strategy that enables students to construct learning for themselves through the exploration phase, the concept development phase, and the concept application phase. All phases are contingent on effective teacher questioning.

Lounge Lizards

Negative school personnel who sometimes take over the teacher's lounge. They are known by their disgruntled attitudes, their incessant gossip, their snipes at others, and their lack of tolerance for anything new or different.

Misconceptions

Faulty understanding of a concept.

No-tolerance Policy (Zero-tolerance Policy)

Zero tolerance—the phrase says exactly what it means: no second chances, no mistakes, no questions, no ifs, ands, or buts. Under many zero-tolerance policies, bringing a plastic knife to school for a lunch is equivalent to bringing a switchblade, and giving a friend aspirin is the same as selling narcotics. Since they are considered equal, so is the punishment—no questions asked.

Performance-contingent Rewards

Rewards that are available only when the student achieves a certain standard (i.e., anyone who makes at least 95 percent on a quiz gets a sticker).

PETA

People for the Ethical Treatment of Animals. *www.peta-online.org*

Public Law 94.142

The Education for All Handicapped Children Act. Passed in 1975, it calls for an Individualized Education Program (IEP) for each child with disabilities. It is a Federal law which requires that all learners with disabilities are educated in the "least restrictive environment."

Reframing

The ability to see events from another perspective.

Resiliency

Ability to recover quickly from setbacks.

Request for Proposals (RFP)

Documents from grant awarding institutions defining their purpose, along with the rules and the process needed in order to obtain their funds. Typically, the institution's evaluators identify those proposals capable of delivering the required results.

Self-efficacy

The belief that one can influence his or her own thoughts and behavior.

Sponge Activity

A short activity designed to "soak up" time that would otherwise be wasted in the classroom. It can be used as "bell ringer" work given at the beginning of a period to engage students when they enter the classroom. Other uses are for the end of class, for unexpected interruptions, or for transitional time during class.

Success-contingent Rewards

Rewards that are given for good performance and might reflect either success or progress towards a goal (e.g., either you make 100 percent on this test or you improve your last score by 5 percent).

Task-contingent Rewards

Rewards that are available to students for merely participating in an activity without regard to any standard of performance (e.g., anyone who turns in a homework paper gets an "A").

Tourette's Syndrome

A chronic, physical disorder of the brain which causes both motor tics and vocal tics. The disorder usually begins before the age of eighteen.

Type A Personality

Manifested behavior characterized by an intense sustained drive to achieve goals and an eagerness to compete. Persons categorized as Type A tend to have a persistent desire for external recognition and advancement.

Type B Personality

Manifested behavior is usually defined as the absence of Type A behavior. Persons categorized as Type B tend to be relaxed, accepting, at ease, patient, and generally content. They are at peace with themselves and others.

Wait Time

Term applied to describe the interval between the time a teacher asks a question and when a learner responds.

"With-it-ness"

A teacher's ability to monitor what is going on in a classroom and be able to act on inappropriate behavior by redirecting it before it is further disruptive.

Zone of Proximal Development

The distance between one's present developmental level and the level of potential future development (e.g., one that is reasonably attainable and yet just far enough beyond easy reach to sustain interest—somewhere between anxiety and boredom).

Bibliography

Armstrong, Thomas. *Awakening Genius in the Classroom.* Alexandria, VA: Association for Supervision and Curriculum Development (ASCD), 1998.

Armstrong, Thomas. *Multiple Intelligences in the Classroom.* 2nd edition. Alexandria, VA: Association for Supervision and Curriculum Development (ASCD), 2000.

Bandura, Albert. Human Agency in Social Cognitive Theory. *American Psychologist* 44 (1175–1184), 1989.

Breeden, Terri, and Emalie Egan. *Positive Classroom Management.* Nashville: Incentive Publications, Inc., 1997.

Brogan, P. A Parent's Perspective: Educating the Digital Generation. *Educational Leadership* 58 (2), 57–59, 2000.

Brophy, Jere E., Ed. *Advances in Research on Teaching.* Greenwich, CT: JAI Press, 1989.

Canter, Lee, and Marlene Canter. *Lee Canter's Assertive Discipline: Positive Behavior Management for Today's Classroom.* Santa Monica: Lee Canter & Associates, 1992.

Canfield, J., and Harold Clive Wells. *100 Ways to Enhance Self-Concept in the Classroom.* 2nd edition. Englewood Cliffs, NJ: Pearson Education, 1994.

Carnegie, Dale. *How to Stop Worrying and Start Living.* NY: Simon & Schuster, 1984.

Chance, P. The Rewards of Learning. *Phi Delta Kappan* 74 (3), 200–207, 1992.

Checkley, K. The First Seven . . . and the Eighth. *Educational Leadership* 55 (1), 8–13, 1997.

Connors, Neila A. *If You Don't Feed the Teachers, They Eat the Students!* Nashville: Incentive Publications, Inc., 2000.

Covey, Stephen R. *The Seven Habits of Highly Effective People.* NY: Free Press, 2004.

Csikszentmihalyi, Mihalyi. *Flow: The Psychology of Optimal Experience.* NY: Harper Perennial, 1991.

Curwin, Richard L., and Allen Mendler. *Discipline with Dignity.* Alexandria, VA: Association for Supervision and Curriculum Development (ASCD), 1988.

DeJong, C., & J. Hawley. Making Cooperative Learning Groups Work. *Middle School Journal* 26 (4), 45–48, 1995.

Forte, Imogene, and Sandra Schurr. *The Cooperative Learning Guide & Planning Pak for Middle Grades.* Nashville: Incentive Publications, Inc., 1992.

Forte, Imogene, and Sandra Schurr. *Standards-Based Math Graphic Organizers*. Nashville: Incentive Publications, Inc., 2001.

Forte, Imogene, and Sandra Schurr. *Standards-Based Science Graphic Organizers*. Nashville: Incentive Publications, Inc., 2001.

Forte, Imogene, and Sandra Schurr. *Standards-Based Social Studies Graphic Organizers*. Nashville: Incentive Publications, Inc., 2001.

Gardner, Howard. *Frames Of Mind: The Theory Of Multiple Intelligences*. 10th edition, NY: Basic Books, 1993.

Gardner, Howard. Reflections on Multiple Intelligences: Myths and Messages. *Phi Delta Kappan* 77 (3), 200–203. 206–209, 1995.

Gregorc, Anthony G. *An Adult's Guide to Style*. Columbia, CT: Gabriel Systems, 1986.

Hatch, T. (1997). Getting Specific about Multiple Intelligences. *Educational Leadership* 54 (6), 26–29, 1997.

Healy, Jean M. *Failure to Connect: How Computers Affect Our Children's Minds—For Better and Worse*. NY: Simon & Schuster, 1998.

Jensen, Eric. *Teaching with the Brain in Mind*. Alexandria, VA: Association for Supervision and Curriculum Development (ASCD), 1998.

Kagan, Jerome M., et al. *Galen's Prophecy: Temperament in Human Nature*. NY: Westview Press, 1995.

Kellough, R. D., and N. G. Kellough. *Middle School Teaching: A Guide to Methods and Resources*. Columbus, OH: Merrill, 1999.

Kohn, Alfie. *Beyond Discipline: From Compliance to Community*. Alexandria, VA: Association for Supervision and Curriculum Development (ASCD), 1996.

Kohn, Alfie. *Punished by Rewards: The Trouble with Gold Stars, Incentive Plans, A's, Praise, and Other Bribes*. Boston: Mariner Books, 1999.

Kounin, Jacob S. *Discipline and Group Management in Classrooms*. Melbourne, FL: Krieger Publishing, 1977.

Lewis, C. C., Schaps, E., and M. S. Watson. The Caring Classroom's Academic Edge. *Educational Leadership* 54 (2). 16–21, 1996.

Lytle, J. H. The Inquiring Manager—Developing New Leadership Structures to Support Reform. *Phi Delta Kappan* 77, 664–670, 1996.

Maslow, Abraham H. *Motivation and Personality*. 3rd edition. NY: HarperCollins, 1987.

Nagy, Allen, and Geraldine Nagy. *How to Raise Your Child's Emotional Intelligence: 101 Ways to Bring Out the Best in Your Children and Yourself.* Bastrop, TX: Heartfelt Publications, 1999.

Newmann, F. M., H. Marks, and A. Gamoran. Authentic Pedagogy: Standards that Boost Student Performance. *Issues in Restructuring Schools* 8, 1–11, 1995.

O'Neil, J. On Emotional Intelligence: A Conversation with Daniel Goleman. *Educational Leadership* 54, (01). 6–11, 1996.

Palmer, Parker J. *To Know As We Are Known: Education as a Spiritual Journey.* San Francisco: Harper San Francisco, 1993.

Piaget, Jean. *To Understand Is to Invent.* NY: Viking Press, 1974.

Purkey, William W. *Self-Concept and School Achievement.* Englewood Cliffs, NJ: Prentice-Hall, 1970.

Randolph, C. H., and C. M. Everston. Images of Management for Learner-Centered Classrooms. *Action in Teacher Education* 16(1) 55–63, 1994.

Sagor, R. Building Resiliency in Students. *Educational Leadership* 54 (2). 38–43, 1996.

Silver, Debbie. Engaging Students in the Learning Cycle. *Principal,* 77 (4), 62–64, 1998.

Sylwester, Robert. *A Celebration of Neurons: An Educator's Guide to the Human Brain.* Alexandria, VA: Association for Supervision and Curriculum Development (ASCD), 1995.

Thompson, Randy, and Dorothy VanderJagt. *Fire UP! for Learning.* Nashville: Incentive Publications, Inc., 2002.

Tomlinson, Carol Ann. *The Differentiated Classroom: Responding To The Needs Of All Learners.* Alexandria, VA: Association for Supervision and Curriculum Development (ASCD), 1999.

Vatterrot, C. Student-Focused Instruction: Balancing Limits with Freedom in the Middle Grades. *Middle School Journal* 28 (2), 28–38, 1995.

Vygotsky, L. S. *Mind In Society: The Development of Higher Psychological Processes.* Cambridge: Harvard University Press, 1980.

Richardson, Virginia., *Ed. Handbook of Research on Teaching.* 4th edition. Englewood Cliffs, NJ: American Educational Research Association, 2001.

Wilson, T. D., and P. W. Linville. Improving Academic Performance of College Freshmen: Attribution Theory Revisited. *Journal of Personality of Social Psychology* 42, 367–376, 1982.

Index

Drumming to the Beat of Different Marchers